Billie Holiday: Jazz Singer
by Meredith Coleman McGee

Foreword by Tawanna Shaunte
Copyright © Jan 14, 2024, Meredith Coleman McGee
Cover design Meredith Coleman McGee
Meredith McGee DBA Meredith Etc

Publisher:
Meredith Etc
1052 Maria Court
Jackson, MS 39204-5151
www.meredithetc.com

Second printing - Hardback & Softcover edition
Printed by Ingram Spark
Black & white interior
Hardcover edition ISBN-13: 978-1-7378843-5-4
Softcover edition ISBN-13: 978-1-7378843-4-7
BIOGRAPHY - Jazz icon
265 pages - Word count: 56,362
64 images and photos
Available on the World Wide Web as an eBook
Cover photo: Billie Holiday, DownBeat, Award Event, 1947
Cover photo: Billie Holiday, NYC Studio picture, 1945

All rights reserved. Submit a written or electronic record requesting material use of this work to the publisher.

Keywords: jazz singer, biography, strange fruit, Billie Holiday, Eleanora Fagan, Harlem, NY, Lester Young

Meredith Coleman McGee

Meredith Etc *a small press*

Blog: meredithetc.com

facebook **Meredith** *Etc*

🐦 **Meredith***etc*

Make comments on the book page:

Billie Holiday | Meredith Etc

Books by Meredith Coleman McGee:
Odyssey
Married to Sin
Midnight Moon
Every Inch Love Will
Billie Holiday: Jazz Singer
James Meredith: Warrior and the America that created him
Children books:
Baby Bubba and Kay
My First Book Series
My Picture Dictionary
Juneteenth: Freedom Day
Nashida: Visits the Mississippi State Capitol
Nashida: Visits the Smith Robertson Museum
Nashida: Visits Mississippi's Old Capitol Museum

Billie Holiday Jazz Singer

by Meredith Coleman McGee

Billie Holiday, 1945, Wikimedia Commons, Public Domain

Meredith Coleman McGee

DEDICATION

Jazz Singer Billie Holiday, Saxophonist Lester Willis Young, Photographer William P. Gottlieb, Library of Congress, Harlem, New York, Baltimore, Maryland, Billie Holiday fans around the world, and the jazz gods here and gone.

Billie Holiday: Jazz Singer

ACKNOWLEDGMENTS

I acknowledge the Central Mississippi Blues Society house band, the Raphael Semmes Quartet, Hal & Mal Restaurant, WJSU Jazz 88.5 @ Jackson State University, Jackson, Mississippi; the interviewees especially: Famous Saxophonist Sonny Rollins and Billie Holiday's goddaughter Billie Jane Lee Lorraine Feather (Lorraine Feather); the proofreaders Alice Paris, Tuskegee, Alabama; Ronald Patterson, Soledad, California; and Loretta Ealy of Jackson, Mississippi. I am thankful to Songstress Tawanna Shaunte, who wrote the foreword, to my life-long friend Alice Smoot who photographed my author pictures, and to all who offered advance praise. Through grace and good will, may music continue to heal the broken hearted and inspire our human dreams.

Meredith Coleman McGee

Meredith Coleman McGee

Billie Holiday Jazz Singer

by Meredith Coleman McGee

Eleanora Harris
Born: April 7, 1915, Philadelphia, PA
Raised: Baltimore, MD

TABLE OF CONTENTS

	PAGES
DEDICATION	iv
ACKNOWLEDGMENTS	v
FOREWORD	ix
ADVANCE PRAISE	xi
INTRODUCTION	xiii

CHAPTERS

ONE	Eleanora	1
TWO	Harlem, New York	19
THREE	Columbia Years	57
FOUR	Decca Years	105
FIVE	Verve Years	132
SIX	1957-1959	149
SEVEN	Aftermath	172
EIGHT	Legacy	186
	ABOUT THE AUTHOR	211

FOREWORD

I was seventeen when I recorded my first song. However, I don't remember what age I was when I initially heard the song *God Bless the Child*. I do remember how it made me feel. I recall paying close attention to the lyrics and melody, which were cheerful, whimsical, and warm. The song offered a soundscape of guidance for independence.

"Them that's got shall get,
Them that's not shall lose
So, the bible said, and it still is news
Mama may have
Papa may have
But God bless the child that's got his own,
that's got his own."

When I was sixteen, my music mentor, Melvin (Housecat) Hendrix, reintroduced me to Billie Holiday's music. He asked, what songs did I desire to learn and sing?" I named a few pieces, including Billie Holiday's *God Bless the Child*. A few weeks later, we visited his friend's home studio, which had an incredible jazz collection. He played Lady Day's recordings from her diverse catalog of songs. Some songs I knew, and some I didn't. However, I enjoyed getting more familiar with the musical classics. What I do remember is that her music was alluring. While listening to her music, I listened closely to the nuisances in her voice and the way she manipulated phrasing and tempo. I discovered that her music and lyrics were her survivors' license. I then understood that is what enchanted her audience.

Not to mention, her vocal style and improvisational skills strongly influenced jazz vocalists and music. Meredith Coleman McGee tells a compelling story of Billie Holiday's ability to interpret the music the way she did. Holiday's turbulent childhood, her abusive relationships, her drug addiction, how the government informants plotted to destroy her career, and the joy she found through true, meaningful, organic friendships molded her musical growth. Also, the emotional joys and pains she shared through her musical creative process were authentic.

Billie Holiday's song *Strange Fruit* is sadly one of America's most potent revolutionary songs. She was arguably the most dynamic artist in music history. Though, she lived an American horror story. Her life and music revealed the incredible amount of tenacity that she had to endure tragedies and triumphs to fight against injustices.

Billie Holiday: Jazz Singer by Meredith Coleman McGee offers incredible scenes into Lady Day's short life that reflects light on society's complexities as a reminder that you don't have to be perfect to create meaningful change.

Tawanna Shaunte, Jazz Vocalist

Advance Praise for *Billie Holiday: Jazz Singer*

I just read *Billie Holiday: Jazz Singer* a biography of Lady Day." What a great book!! The author covers so much information in this book. It reads easily, as well. I learned so much from this wonderful biography and feel like I met Billie Holiday! All the great pictures are just a bonus!!

Chris Gill, Central Mississippi Blues Society, Musician Member, Performer

Billie Holiday: Jazz Singer is an excellent, informative, inspirational, and musically historically accurate book which is a must read for jazz lovers.

Ronald Shelton, Pensacola Jazz Society, Member & Jazz Music Collector

Meredith Coleman McGee's portrait of American icon Billie Holiday is intimate and unflinching, as it details her life and music in the context of 20th century race relations, drug use and abuse, rackets and the jazz business, and complicated relations with her family and friends. As an introduction to the great singer's place in history and the present, it's highly relatable to readers now.

Howard Mandel, Author, Editor & President, Jazz Journalists Association

I just finished reading *Billie Holiday: Jazz Singer*. What a wonderful and refreshing look at her. Her life was chronicled in such a refreshing way; the lows and highs of her life were given true meaning, which showed the promise music provides to healing.

Malcolm Sheppard, President, Central Mississippi Blues Society

As Pluto once said, "...Books give a soul to the universe, wings to the mind, flight to the imagination and life to everything." I found Meredith Coleman McGee's Billie *Holiday: Jazz Singer,* a biography of Lady Day, to be an extraordinary and exceptional book which shares the incredible life of Billie Holiday. May the gardenias in the garden continue to bloom for the next generation of artists who have a passion for the arts and revolution.

Arcell Cabuag, Director of Education, Restoration Dance Youth Ensemble Artistic Director

Meredith Coleman McGee's scholarly book, *Billie Holiday: Jazz Singer,* is a loving and sincere reflection of the genius of Lady Day whose contributions to jazz are unparalleled. This intimate work which beautifully summarizes the struggles and accomplishments of this incredible artist spans her life from childhood through her 30-year career to her untimely death in 1959. This book honors how her musical interpretations and inspirations changed our world forever. While reading, I heard Holiday's classic sultry voice. This book is a must read for fans of Billie Holiday and Jazz music scholars.

Dr. Laura Petillo, Music Programs Manager, Count Basie Center for the Arts

Billie Holiday: Jazz Singer

INTRODUCTION

I became a fan of Billie Holiday, known famously as Lady Day, at age 15, in 1978, in the 10th grade. My older brother Bobby, age 16 and a half, a music enthusiast, who later became a DJ at the CB Club in the Black entertainment Strip in Jackson, Mississippi, introduced me to Billie Holiday. The old clubs where Stardust and Dorsey's once stood, and Estelle's, the one soul food eatery, are gone now. Today, the entertainment strip which blossomed for decades was crushed by the effects of gun violence during the Crack Cocaine epidemic; the district now contains a series of vacant lots. Nationally other Black entertainment business districts have disintegrated in the past 50 years.

Since Billie Holiday's heyday, over 64 years ago, when she sold out concert seats at Carnegie Hall, established in 1891, by Steel Tycoon Andrew Carnegie, this venue has flourished. In 1947, her concert tickets were on sale at the Carnegie Box Office, Colony Record Shop, 52nd & B' way; and Flaps Record Shop, 125th St. & 7th Ave. Concert seats ranged from $4.00 to $2.25. Today, Carnegie Hall concert goers pay $120 to $3,000 per seat.

Carnegie Hall on 7th Street between 56th and 57th Streets in NYC has been standing for over 130 years. The Apollo Theater in Harlem, New York which launched amateur contests in 1934 was an extension of the Chitlin' Circuit; it has been standing 89 years and counting. Billie Holiday debuted at the Apollo that year as a rising star and a paid singer. The Royal Theater on Pennsylvania Avenue in Baltimore where Billie Holiday grew up was one of five theaters for Black entertainment during legal segregation. The facility was demolished in 1971 on the eve of its 50th anniversary. The Regal Theater, which opened in 1928 in the Bronzeville community on the southside of Chicago was one of the first premiere complexes in America available to Black audiences. The Regal Theater ran 40 years - until 1968. The facility was torn down in 1973.

Of the five largest theaters, Howard Theater in Washington, D.C., which ran amateur contests in the 1930s for Black people has remained an entertainment spot for over a century. Billie Holiday performed in the major theaters. She also sang in the lesser-known clubs on the Chitlin' Circuit, especially after her drug conviction in 1947 which revoked her Cabaret license and her ability to perform in the jazz clubs in NYC. From age 19 to age 23, she was the featured singer with the Benny Goodman Band, the Count Basie Band, the Artie Shaw Band, and at Café Society.

Billie Holiday was born Eleanora Harris, on April 7, 1915, in Philadelphia, Pennsylvania out of wedlock to teenage parents. She grew up in Baltimore, Maryland, the birthplace of both her parents and her fore parents, close to the neighborhood where the famed orator, writer, author, and abolitionist Frederick Douglass (1817-1895) spent his last moments, in 1838, as a slave.

Jazz developed around 1910 in Storyville - the redlight district in New Orleans where wealthy madams who ran brothels hired local musicians to entertain guests in lavish mansion ballrooms and palace parlors.

On Eleanora's second birthday, jazz was thriving in Baltimore. Early in her life, Eleanora gravitated to music and discovered a happy place. As young as six, she laid on the floor in front of the Victrola and sang along with the comforting voices sprouting out of the speakers.

After completing the 5th grade, Eleanora dropped out of

Billie Holiday: Jazz Singer

school and ran errands for a brothel which was ripe with music. Between errands, Eleanora paused to sing along with the recordings of Louis Armstrong and Bessie Smith. Louis had a mellow sound plus he was a skilled scat singer. Bessie Smith was the Empress of the Blues and one the highest paid Black entertainers in the nation. Louis Armstrong was one of the most influential figures of the jazz genre. Louis, a protégé of King Oliver, played the second cornet in King Oliver's Creole Band.

Jazz was an integral part of the Black community when my father, Robert "Bobby Joe" was born in 1939. He played trumpet at Carver High School in Gadsden, Alabama. He played jazz, blues, soul, and gospel music around the house in the 1960s when we were young. We were dancing and bobbing our heads as soon as we could stand on our feet. By age 13, my brother had collected albums by the Ohio Players, Prince, McKinley Mitchel, Jimmie Hendrix, Billie Holiday, The Gap Band, and others. Bobby took every dollar he could rake and scrap to local music stores. He signed his nickname "Bobby" on each album cover. He knew who wrote which songs, which instrument each band member played, and which record labels produced the albums.

One evening, Bobby said smiling with a deep look of excitement on his face, "They say Billie Holiday ruined her voice using drugs. But she sounded better. Listen to this." Then, Bobby played music recorded by Billie Holiday in the 1950s including *Fine and Mellow*. I was hooked. *God Bless the Child* was talking directly to me. "Mama may have, papa may have, but God bless the child that's got his own." The lyrics were my vision of one day owning my own home and being the boss of it. By then, mama was bossing our house. Daddy was gone.

Bobby and I went to the school library at Hinds Agricultural High School to research the greatest jazz vocalist on record. One of the Librarians, Mrs. Alma Fisher, helped us find articles on Billie Holiday, who was quoted saying, "Drugs and alcohol will only kill you slowly." The article noted that Billie Holiday desired to share the perils of drugs and alcohol with youth. I expected to read about her fame and fortune. As far as we knew, when we had a chance to smoke reefer, everyone laughed and laughed and had fun.

Mrs. Fisher read our expressions and said, "Hum,' you didn't expect her to say that did you?" I did not expect Lady Day to make such a profound declaration. She said, 'kill' as in self-destruct.

Billie Holiday's warning went flat over our heads. In fact, not long afterward, Bobby heard about a weed dealer named Blind, who sold reefer in match boxes for $5 in Virden Addition between Northside Dr., Bailey Ave., and Livingston Road. We collected the money, counted it, and Bobby walked from our street off Watkins Drive to score the reefer. Blind pulled grass from his yard, filled the matchbox up, and beat us out of the money we pooled together.

We walked to Blind's house multiple times to get a refund or our product. Every day, someone answered the door and said "Blind just left. Come back." After going back and forth and hearing a new excuse by the same or different family member, we gave up. Retaliation was not an option. As the saying goes, "We charged that $5 to the game." The matchbox incident was our first lesson about the streets. Eleanora was younger than us when she faced the wheeling and dealings of the streets. Everyone has a story. Bets on, you will enjoy the story I wrote about Lady Day.

Billie Holiday: Jazz Singer

The streets are full of people making quick cash. The hustler's anthem is *a mark is a mark*. Four or five teenagers from our block were Blind's mark. Hustlers are cruel. Elenora grew up in the fast lane in Baltimore in Pigtown in the 1920s. In her mother's absence, Eleanora snuck out of the window, alone, late at night, and walked to the party scene where blues and jazz music played and where slick talkers, con artists, pimps, and tricksters dwelled.

Her father Clarence started playing the banjo for tips in Baltimore on the same streets. She was fascinated with her father's work and obsessed with Louis Armstrong and Bessie Smith. She saw a different world as an underage participant of Baltimore's nightlife. She was brave and hardheaded. By age 15, she had formed her own singing style which was slow and soft. Audiences loved the sound of the pie faced, 200 lb. 5'7" teen.

However, a few listeners did not appreciate her style. But she stuck to her grits and her unique singing style. She obtained her musical break at age 18 in Harlem where she moved people in the audience to tears. She was an intimate entertainer and vocalist who made people feel she was singing to them.

Practically, every book and source I read on Billie Holiday from *Strange Fruit* to *Lady Day: The Many Faces of Billie Holiday* discussed her addiction as a part of her demise. To my knowledge there were no heroin addicts in our southern Black community in Mississippi in the 1970s. But heroin and hard drugs let loose among jazz musicians including Charlie Parker, John Coltrane, Miles Davis, and others. Saxophonist Sonny Rollins said youth who followed Charlie Parker started using heroin. Sonny recalled that Charlie hated that his followers picked up his destructive habit. White stars such as Judy Garland, who played Dorothy in the *Wizard of Oz* fell prey to addiction too.

During the WWII era the dangers of hard drugs were not widely known. Experts propose heroin is a drug which is practically impossible to kick. Some did. Many did not. Sonny Rollins got clean and stayed clean. He played his saxophone past age 80.

By the time users look for a cure it is too late to find one. Drugs and alcohol can damage bodily organs. Charlie Parker died at age 34. Billie Holiday died at age 44. Judy Garland died at age 47. Billie Holiday was targeted by drug agents under the guise of the War on Drugs. But law enforcement rarely pursued white public figures and entertainers.

Bobby and I saw the 1972 movie *Lady Sings the Blues* featuring Diana Ross and Billy Dee Williams in the late 1970s. For me, the movie portrayed Billie Holiday as *the best that ever did it*. Richard Prior played the piano man. His role was the opposite of Teddy Wilson. Lester Young and Clarance Holiday were omitted completely. Billy Dee's character turned big bad Louis McKay into a saint. Ha' Ha.'

Some books on Billie Holiday in the past 30 years were based on research via interviews recorded in the 1970s by Journalist Linda Lipnack Huehl who planned to write a biography but died before she could finish. She interviewed Count Basie, Tony Bennett, Jo Jones, and others who gave candid interviews about the late Billie Holiday. Several interviews were featured in the 2019 documentary *Billie*.

My late husband Will and I watched *The United States v. Billie Holiday* in 2021 staring Andra Day and directed by Lee

Billie Holiday: Jazz Singer

Daniels. I introduced Will to Billie Holiday 25 years ago when we moved into our home in South Jackson, Mississippi. He grew fond of the duet *Sweet Hunk o' Trash* by Billie Holiday featuring Louis Armstrong. Several lyrics are below:

You don't add up to much.
Ain't got that glamour touch... Billie Holiday sang.

Look out there, mama.
You carrying me a little too fast. Louis Armstrong replied.

You're my good for nothin.'
Sweet hunk o' trash. Billie Holiday sang

Will and I played our collection of music religiously on wax, cassette tape, and on CD. And I still do. I can remember like it was yesterday, Will watching me sing *Now or Never* by Billie Holiday before we married.

Several lyrics are as follows:

It's gotta' be yes or no.
It's either you stay or go.
You can't leave me on the shelf.
You gotta' commit yourself.
It's either you will baby or won't fall in love with me...

I stood on my feet 5'3.5" and sang my heart out. I was unstoppable. After I turned 59, I pulled out my college paper, *So Much Jazz: Billie Holiday* which I submitted for my history course July 23, 1986, at the University of West Florida. At that time, I interned for Allbritton & Gant. I am grateful to Attorney Fred Gant because he allowed his legal secretary to type my paper so I could submit it on time.

Meredith Coleman McGee

During the summer of 2022, I retyped my college paper and started reading and researching the life and times of the late Great Billie Holiday. What I wrote back then was tiny compared to this full biography. I have advanced from a misinformed fan into an informed fan. The movie *Lady Sings the Blues* only touches the surface of the life and times of Billie Holiday. For 44 years, I have been a fan of Lady Day. From the perspective of a fan, I am sharing the magic moments of a big jazz life well lived.

Finally, I experienced enough in life to understand Lady Day's message about fast living and the consequences of addiction to add a new spin on the Billie Holiday story. Her story offers diverse lessons. Billie Holiday warned Etta James. But Etta James lived long enough – 74 years – to get that monkey off her back, to sing at a Jazz Festival in New Orleans seated on a stool, and to record a final album which introduced Will and I and another generation to her art. Yes, Beyonce's portrayal of Etta James in *Cadillac Records* did the rest.

Billie Holiday admitted in her autobiography, *Lady Sings the Blues,* which was published January 1, 1956, the dangers of drug use; she did not blame anyone for her addiction. She took full responsibility for her choices. She learned while touring in Europe in the 1950s that addiction was treated as a disease abroad, while it was criminalized in the United States. The modern Opioid Crisis changed the landscape on how addiction is treated in America. However, drugs are very lethal.

Today, the warning to youth is: one drug experience can be one's last experience. There is no come back for far too many; second chances have become slim to none in a society where drugs are laced with Fentanyl and other fatal synthetic opioids. Too many are gone too soon – Coolio, DMX, Whitney Houston, Amy Winehouse, Prince, Michael Jackson...

Lady Day died July 17, 1959, at age 44. Her story is over the top. By age 24, she had graced the cover of *Time* for her singular voice. She was the late, great, innovative, jazz singer. Read *Billie Holiday: Jazz Singer*, a story about a jazz superstar, who set Jazz on fire, in 1933, in Harlem, New York, over 90 years ago.

ONE

Eleanora

Today, Billie Holiday is one of the most celebrated female jazz artists. Columbia Records Producer John Hammond discovered 18-year-old Billie Holiday in Harlem in 1933. He declared, "Holiday was fresh and new.[1]" When John Hammond first laid his eyes on Billie Holiday at the end of prohibition in a speakeasy in Harlem, she was singing without a microphone from table to table the same lyrics differently. John Hammond had never met a singer who improvised lyrics. He said, "She sounded like an improvising horn player[2]."

Billie Holiday was the first Black woman whose image was featured in *Life* and the *New York Times*. She was the first widely known Black female protest singer in America. She sang *Strange Fruit* 20 years before the Civil Rights moment took flight. She was a War on Drugs suspect 20 years before Pres. Richard Nixon launched a War on Drugs aimed at arresting Vietnam protestors and Black militant groups like the Black Panthers.

Four white males: George Washington, 1st USA President, Founding Father; Thomas Jefferson, Founding Father; Theodore Roosevelt, 26th President; and Abraham Lincoln, 16th President are memorialized with face carvings on Mount Rushmore in Keystone, South Dakota. In contrast, imagine somewhere in the sky the faces of jazz gods:

Meredith Coleman McGee

Louis Armstrong, Duke Ellington, Billie Holiday, Lester Young, Art Tatum, Ella Fitzgerald, Sarah Vaughan... Wayne Shorter and Admad Jamal joined the cloud collage in 2023. The jazz gods influence has touched the world. Jazz evolved from Swing, to Bebop, to Cool and beyond. Jazz has many ancestors. Billie Holiday is a great jazz goddess.

The incomparable Billie Holiday was born, at 2:30 a.m. April 7, 1915, to Sara Julia Harris, age 19 and Clarence Earnest Halliday, age 17, out of wedlock, at Philadelphia General Hospital in Philadelphia, Pennsylvania.[3] The hospital was formerly a poorhouse and served as a mental health facility at the onset of WWI. At the time of Eleanora's birth, Philadelphia General Hospital was the city's only public hospital. By the height of the Great Migration after WWII, the hospital was the primary medical center for Black people, particularly, Black women.

Philadelphia General Hospital 1913, Library of Congress

Sara was the illegitimate daughter of Charles Fagan, a fair skinned middle-class Negro who lived in the Sandtown-

Billie Holiday: Jazz Singer

Winchester subdivision (Sandtown) in West Baltimore, Maryland. Sara unofficially adopted her father's surname and adjusted her first name and went by Sadie Fagan giving herself a legitimacy she lacked in real time. Based on census records Clarence was the son of Nelson Halliday with Mary Johnson Halliday, who married in 1895 in Baltimore three years before Clarence's birth.

Sandtown was known as Baltimore's Harlem during the city's jazz peak. Famous performers like Duke Ellington, Chick Webb, Louis Armstrong, Cab Calloway, and Diana Ross performed there through the 1960s. The assassination of Martin Luther King Jr. in Memphis on April 4, 1968, triggered rioting in Sandtown and over 100 other U.S.A. cities. Sandtown experienced economic depression following the eight days of rioting.

National Black figureheads were assassinated back-to-back – Medgar Evers, 1963; Malcolm X, 1965, Martin Luther King Jr., 1968, and Chairman Fred Hampton, 1969. Each loss killed the hope of rising for an entire people. Black people converted their rage into rioting. Therefore, other Black districts declined. *We couldn't win for losing*. Forty-seven years later, the negligent police custody death of Freddie Gray, in 2015 sparked riots, business disruptions, business destruction, and more economic depression. The old Black entertainment and business districts in West Baltimore have been replaced with economic inactivity and community blight. Sandtown's unemployment rate for residents ages 16 to 64 is double the rates in other communities. Poverty and crime became close cousins.

Before Eleanora's birth, Sadie moved in with her father and stepmother, Martha, who were devout Catholics.

Sadie attended mass and followed the rules until she engaged in a brief affair with Clarence, whom she met after he performed at a musical gig at a Carnival in Baltimore. Though only 16, Clarence was immersed in the nightlife, playing the banjo for tips, and earning 50¢ per gig.[4] Clarence started entertaining small audiences in Baltimore when he was 14 years old. He and his childhood friend, Elmer Snowden, played with jazz bands in Baltimore before their musical talents garnered them national notoriety.

Sadie was a good girl, who went to school, mass, and to social events. However, good Catholic girls were not supposed to fornicate with boys. When Sadie revealed she was pregnant, Martha obtained consent from Charles and initiated getting Sadie, who was pregnant with a musical gift to the world, kicked out of the house for bringing shame to the family.

Interestingly, Sadie was illegitimate too; she was living breathing proof of Charles immoral discretions with Sadie's mother Sussie Harris. As the Jamaican proverb noted, "Finger nebber say, "look here," him say "look dere[5]." Sadie's fruit did not fall too far from her mother Sussie's tree. Sussie was 19 years old, and Charles was 26 when Sara was conceived out of wedlock.

After Sadie announced her pregnancy, Charles and his wife went one step further and banned Sadie and Eleanora from their home. However, Charles had a soft spot for his daughter and granddaughter. He played both ends of the stick. He quietly gave Sadie money to show his daughter he cared while keeping peace at home by abiding by his wife's "ban the sinful child and grandchild" rule. The 1930 census listed Mattie Fagan, a native of Virginia, as the second wife of Charles Fagan.

Sadie travelled to Philadelphia and gave birth to her daughter and named her Eleanora. One source reported that her given name was spelled Elinore. Sadie returned to East Baltimore and she and her baby moved in with Sadie's maternal family. From time to time, Clarence looked up Sadie and visited with her and his daughter. Sadie grew to love Clarence, but she could not persuade him *to do right*. Sadie walked to spots where Clarence was around town and tried to engage him to be a father to their only child.

Eleanora spent part of her childhood in Pigtown, a slum district in Baltimore. Pigtown borders present day Martin Luther King Jr. Boulevard on the east; Monroe Street on the west; Russell Street on the southern border; and Pratt Street to the north. Baseball icon Babe Ruth, who was around the age of Sadie and Clarence, grew up in a two-parent household in Pigtown.

Eleanora was well acquainted with her grandfather Charles' side of the family. She often heard stories about her grandmother's former life as a slave in Virginia. Eleanora understood racism through her grandmother's experience and life itself.

In 1920, Sadie, age 24 and Eleanora, age 4, lived with Sadie's sister Eva Miller, age 33 and her husband Robert Miller, age 43. The couple's young children, Charles, age 3 and Dorothy, an infant, also lived in the house. Sadie was employed as an operator at a Shirt Factory. The Millers had White and Italian neighbors. Several Italian neighbors were skilled laborers working as tailors and pressers at a Clothing Factory. One was a shoemaker.

Another one worked at a Macaroni Factory. Baltimore had other industries including an Ammunition Plant. The nearby Brickyard employed many males. Clothing manufacturing was the number one industry in Maryland. Canning was the second largest industry.

Eleanora's family roots in Maryland predate the American Civil War. Charles Fagan's mother Rebecca, born in 1852, was also a Maryland native. Rebecca, employed as a washing woman, was listed in the 1870 census as a Mulatto, widow head of household. In the 1880 census Charles, age 11, was enrolled in school. He was listed as a Mulatto too. Three younger siblings were listed. Based on findings in *Lady Sings the Blues*, Eleanora's Grandfather Charles was part Irish. His father immigrated from Ireland.

Sadie's mother, Sussie Harris, was born in June of 1876 in Maryland. Sadie's relatives with the surname Harris, aunts, uncles, and siblings were listed in her household: Mary, 1886; Henry, 1887; George W. 1897; Sara 1898, and Maggie E. 1899. Clarence's parents Nelson Halliday, born 1856 and Mary, born 1865 were also Maryland natives.

Sadie chose not to identify herself with her Harris lineage. Sadie went by her father's surname Fagan to legitimize her birth. In those days, there was a negative stigma attached to being born out of wedlock. Illegitimate children were called 'bastard children.' Bastard means polluted. Children born outside the home may be excluded from the family inheritance and even from obtaining social security benefits, etc.

From 1810 to 1860, Maryland had the largest population of free Black people in the union. Slavery officially ended in Maryland in 1864. Baltimore Black people worked with whites in integrated companies during the Civil War. Free Black people in Baltimore were progressive; they were active in the Underground Railroad and helped slaves gain safe passage to the north. However, the White Power Structure of Maryland, a neighboring state of Virginia, were sympathetic to the Confederacy. White Baltimoreans supported slavery and incited rioting in the city in 1861. President Lincoln ordered Union troops to occupy the city to quell the riots.

Free Black people in Baltimore made great strides in the city prior to the Civil War. Free Black people organized churches, schools, and benevolent societies. The NAACP'S Baltimore Branch was formed in 1912. Black culture flourished. The Baltimorean Black working class and the business class spurred economic growth.

The Black press was present. Zora Neale Hurston, who became a famous Black writer, graduated from Morgan State College in Baltimore in 1918 three years after Eleanora's birth. A century later, Hurston's manuscript *Barracoon: The Story of the Last 'Black Cargo'* was published and became a bestselling literary book in 2018 due to the efforts of famed Author Alice Walker, who is best known for her book *The Color Purple*.

Pennsylvania Ave flourished with jazz and the arts and was a key stop for Black entertainers and an extension of the Chitlin Circuit. The term Chitlin Circuit was derived from the term Chitterlings which was the bottom food staple enslaved Africans were forced to eat during the institution of slavery. Chitterlings – pork intestines are an inferior food source which must be cleaned thoroughly – in seven of more rinses and a light boiling - to remove the feces. Half cleaned Chitterlings can cause food poisoning.

In the early 1950s, Mississippi Blues icon Bobby Rush earned $3 per night entertaining small crowds in Chicago at the Squeeze Inn in the Chitlin' Circuit. Bobby Rush and his band were paid in dollar bills and in hamburgers. "We ate three of the hamburgers and sold the others[6]," Bobby Rush declared. The Chitlin' Circuit was the bottom of the come up for Black entertainers. For Bobby Rush and others, small beginnings became big endings.

Clarence Holiday was drafted into WWI (1914-1918) when Eleanora was a toddler. During his tour, he learned how to play the guitar. Unfortunately, Clarence was exposed to mustard gas which weakened his lungs.

In 1920, Sadie saved enough money to move from East Baltimore to North Baltimore where she met Phil Gough, a dock worker. Phil and Sadie fell in love and the two married that year. Eleanora was five years old when her mother married Phil Gough. Phil gave the family stability. Phil was Eleanora's first father figure. By age 7, Eleanora's parents separated rendering Sadie a single struggling parent again. Sadie worked long hours and Eleanora was often left in the care of her maternal relatives, who believed Eleanora felt abandoned and acted out because she resented being deserted by Sadie.

After his military tour, Clarence observed Eleanora's toughness. She was tomboyish. She played hard ball, could box a little, loved skating, and didn't mind fist fighting. Clarence nicknamed his non-conventional daughter, "Bill."

According to Billie Holiday's autobiography *Lady Sings the Blues*, during Elementary school, Eleanora worked as a babysitter to earn money; on Saturdays she scrubbed steps to help rake in funds. In Sadie's absence, Eleanora lived under the care of her cousin Ida. Eleanora slept in the same bed with two cousins: Elsie and Henry. Henry often wet the bed and denied it. Eleanora was blamed and whipped for Henry's bed wetting.

Baltimore, Maryland step scrubber - Library of Congress. Workers scrubbed the white marble steps every Saturday.

In Eleanora's youth, William Llewellyn Wilson was the prominent Black music teacher at Frederick Douglass High School, established 1883, the second oldest public high school in the nation for Black people. Wilson trained the city's jazz greats including Blanche Calloway, the older sister of Cab Calloway, a famous jazz entertainer. Wilson taught his students how to read music. But Billie Holiday and her musical idols Bessie Smith, who was as big as it got in blues; and Louis Armstrong, who was as big as it got in jazz, could not read music. Music dwelled in their souls deep in their hearts. Billie Holiday's admirers said her voice could swing to the beat like an instrument.

Eleanora completed the 5th grade in the Baltimore Public School system. On January 5, 1925, the authorities picked Eleanora up for truancy. She was sent to the House of the Good Shepherds reform school where she was given a new name – Marge as a symbol of God bestowing a new and better life for Eleanora.

Eleanora was released; yet more trouble followed when a 40-year-old male neighbor, known as Mr. Dick (Wilbert Rich), raped, or attempted to rape Eleanora when she was 11 years old. One account noted that Sadie and a police officer saved Eleanora, but the case ended up in juvenile court. Dick was sentenced to three months in jail for carnal knowledge of a minor.

Eleanora was punished too. A judge ordered Eleanora Gough to live at the House of Good Shepherd, a Catholic home for Black wayward girls, until she turned age 21. The facility was founded in 1864 by the Catholic order of the Sisters of the Good Shepherd to help women and girls in crisis. Sadie fought the judge's order and obtained Eleanora's early release. Eleanora was released to Sadie in February of 1927 by order of habeas corpus.

Sadie and Eleanora became boarders in the home of Viola Green. Viola's son Freddie recalled that Eleanora listened to music on a home record player and when she was 11 or 12 years old, she often walked around the house singing. In her spare time, Eleanora read Romance magazines.

Popular music of the day included blues and jazz tunes which were not suitable for the ears of young girls. Sadie protested. But Eleanora, who lived in a rough neighborhood, saw the life the lyrics depicted. Eleanora was cursing, fussing, drinking, and creeping. Songs Eleanora heard at age 11 and 12 are as follows:

Sugar Foot Stomp by Fletcher Henderson and His Orchestra
Sweet Georgia Brown by Ethel Waters and Her Ebony Four
Lost Your Head Blues by Bessie Smith
I'm Wild About That Thing by Bessie Smith
Me and My Gin by Bessie Smith
Wild Man Blues by Louis Armstrong and His Hot Five
Willie the Weeper by Louis Armstrong and His Hot Five
Come Back Sweet Papa by Louis Armstrong & His Hot Five

Bessie Smith was telling grown woman stories through her music. The lyrics to Bessie Smith's songs were telling. Excerpts of *Lost Your Head Blues* by Bessie Smith and *Me and My Gin* lyrics by Bessie Smith are below:

Lost Your Head Blues by Bessie Smith

I was with you, baby, when you didn't have a dime
I was with you, baby, when you didn't have a dime
Now since you got plenty money
You have thrown your good girl down[7]

Me and My Gin by Bessie Smith

Stay away from me 'cause I'm in my sin
Stay away from me 'cause I'm in my sin
If this place gets raided, it's me and my gin

Don't try me nobody, oh, you will never win
Don't try me nobody 'cause you will never win
I'll fight the army, navy, just me and my gin[8]

Meredith Coleman McGee

Bessie Smith, 1933, Library of Congress

Come Back Sweet Papa lyrics by Louis Armstrong

Billie Holiday: Jazz Singer

Chorus:
Won't you please come back
Cause the sound of your voice has got me
wondering why I'm so distracted.
So, won't you please, please come back
I'll be waiting next time that you call to discuss how
you've acted
Confession, come on baby

Now, was it her,
That sold you kisses at St. Patrick's last bazaar
Or the one drank more whiskey
And drove off in a brand-new car

Or the widow who was weeping
For the husband that she lost
Or the one at the reception
Who was dancing with the dogs...[9]

The Blues is a living and breathing story. Eleanora, a preteen, started sneaking out the window going to the club scene and party houses in Baltimore. She could look around and see real stories connected to song lyrics. While Sadie was away, Eleanora was walking the streets with friends, smoking cigarettes and reefer and drinking. Eleanora loved music and dancing and listening to her musical idols - Louis Armstrong and Bessie Smith.

Eleanora performed cleaning chores for Alice Dean, a madam in Baltimore and she ran arrands for the prostitutes who lived in Alice's establishment. Eleanora listened and sang jazz and blues playing on the Victrola record player in the parlor.

In those days, few Black families, who earned $25 to $30 per week, could afford a Victrola. The price of Victrola's ranged from $25 to $1,500. Alice Dean needed a Victrola because playing the latest music was one of the benefits provided to customers in whorehouses; music was emersed in the environment of brothels, good time houses, and music halls; therefore, music was always in Eleanora's ears. Eleanora was all over the place. Eventually people noticed her talent and she started singing in front of small crowds.

Louis Armstrong portrait in 1938 by William P. Gottlieb

Sadie worried about Eleanora being around boys when she was growing up. Sadie declared, "You ain't got no father. I work so hard. Please don't make the same mistake I made.[10]" Ida used to accuse Eleanora of being fast. However, Eleanora claimed Ida and the grown folks on her block should have been worried about one of the saintly girls on the block, instead of her because the nice girls were having sexual relations with the boys and married men.

Silent Film Movie Star Billie Dove, Library of Congress

Like most adolescents, Eleanora was mischievous. She used to shoplift white socks from the local five-and-dime stores. She crawled in the back way at the movies to save her dime. She watched all the Billie Dove movies. Eleanora even tried to fix her hair like Billie Dove. Eleanora had silky hair which she inherited from her Irish ancestors. She used to hang around local boys, play marbles, and shoot dice with them.

National Photo Co. Collection (Library of Congress) 1921

By age 12, Eleanora befriended Ethel Moore, an older woman who owned a good time house at 20 Bond Street in Baltimore in Fell's Point in the waterfront red-light district. Ethel became a surrogate older sister who schooled Eleanora about street life.

One Baltimorean, Pony Kane, remembered seeing Eleanora at Alice Dean's bordello. According to Pony

Kane, Eleanora sang to tricks, who requested the "singing girl." Eleanora was also known to go from house to house with pianists singing ragtime tunes. She also sang frequently at good time houses in East Baltimore on Bethel and Pratt, Central and Pratt, and Baltimore and Pratt.

Eleanora witnessed "musician battles," wherein musicians put up a few dollars as a wager to see which piano player, horn player, or banjo player pleased the crowd more. The session was settled by the loudest applause. The party goers often jammed all night drinking bootlegged whiskey, smoking weed, and eating fish and ribs. Most underage party goers, except Eleanora, attended school the next morning. After her ordeal with Mr. Dick, Eleanora dropped out of school.

By age 12, Eleanora was well known in Baltimore's redlight district. Her childhood friends recalled that the best dressed hustlers in Baltimore used to come in the neighborhood to get Eleanora so she could sing in one of the good time houses or on the waterfront. Eleanora was an underage, well-known singing girl. She developed her own singing style in Baltimore through her regular singing routines. Eleanora briefly sang in the compulsory Catholic Mass every day in the Catholic chapel at the House of the Good Shepherd where she was disciplined in formal singing including the practice of phrasing words and using defined diction.

Baltimore pimp Skinny Davenport recalled in his interview about Eleanora Fagan's childhood with journalist Linda Lipnack Huehl, "And then she liked to be with the boys." When asked why Eleanora liked being with the boys, he replied, "Yeah, well we all had a lot of money." He added, "She used to sing every night[11]."

Davenport confirmed that Eleanora sang nightly, although he did not specify those to whom she sang. Eleanora did not have any key male figures in her life to protect from the streets and from being exploited, but she had close friends and older female protectors in her village.

Eleanora got in trouble again for being a juvenile delinquent. Sadie challenged the record which charged that Eleanora did not have a guardian. The judge's ruling was reversed. In 1927, Sadie moved to New York to find work and to earn enough money to reunite with Eleanora. Coincidentally, 29-year-old Clarence married 29-year-old Fannie Taylor in Manhattan, New York that year. It is ironic that Sadie moved to New York after Clarence settled there. Sadie pointedly reminded Clarence that he was the father of a girl named Eleanora. Sadie wanted Clarence to accept his responsibility as the father of their child. She tried extremely hard. She followed him to New York.

Harlem, NY, 1935, Courtesy Library of Congress

Billie Holiday: Jazz Singer

Two

Harlem, New York

Young Eleanora, age 13, arrived in Harlem, New York on the train to reunite with her mother, in 1928, on the heels of the Great Depression. Black people originally moved to Harlem near Lenox Avenue after the 1893 economic panic which caused, bank failures, high unemployment, and large apartment vacancy rates in Harlem. At the urging of Phillip Payton Jr., a Black realtor, property owners leased apartments to large groups of Black tenants in 1904 and 1905. Payton is known famously as 'The Father of Harlem' for his role in improving tenement structures for Black tenants.

Harlem was incorporated in 1660 by the Dutch as New Haarlem after the Dutch city, Haarlem, North Holland in the Netherlands in Europe. Harlem is known as Upper Manhattan which takes its name from the Manhattans, a native Indian tribe who inhabited the area long before European settlement and before German, Italian, Caribbean, and Jewish immigrants arrived in mass numbers. Harlem borders the Hudson River on the west, 155th Street on the north, Fifth Avenue on the east, and Central Park North on the south.

By WWI most residential and commercial property in Harlem was occupied by Black people. The 1920s ushered in Black intellectuals including Allain Locke, Langston Hughes, Richard Wright, Nella Larsen, James Weldon Johnson, and Zora Neale Hurston launching the Harlem Renaissance. Marcus Mosiah Garvey's Pan African Movement promoting Black independence featuring mass meetings, parades, and membership drives was rooted in Harlem. Harlem became the Black Mecca of the United States of America. New Yorkers call Harlem 'Uptown.'

Panic - scene drawn by Charles Broughton depicting the New York Stock Exchange, Friday, morning, May 5, 1893

Billie Holiday: Jazz Singer

Harlem Nightclub Map, E. Simms Campbell, Negro illustrator

The period in history known as the New Negro Movement or the Harlem Renaissance was centered around an intellectual and cultural revival of Black art, dance, music, fashion, literature, theater, politics, and scholarship. Eleanora saw the club lights; she saw the stars; she saw the well to do; she saw the not so well to do; she saw black, and she saw white; she saw police brutality and discrimination. Eleanora never imagined she would become a major player in the new cultural reform as a great jazz lady. But she did.

The good times of the roaring 1920s were vanishing when Sadie and Eleanora settled in Harlem. But mother and daughter were determined to survive. They did. Sadie was an experienced house cleaner. Technically, the two escaped poverty in Black Baltimore and were greeted by poverty in Black Harlem. When cleaning and boarding in middle class households was not available, they pursued other options to eat, to sleep, and to live. Mother and daughter lived through it all – the good times – the troubled times – the bread-and-butter times – and the easier times.

Sadie found Eleanora a domestic job. Eleanora despised being a maid. She discussed her grievances with friends, and they ventured toward the shining bright night lights. Eleanora's singing roots started in Baltimore and resumed in Harlem. Eleanora, age 13, sang at house parties and rent parties in New York. Then, she started singing at small clubs.

Welfare Island, New York, New York. Library of Congress

Sadie and Eleanora briefly became boarders at Florence Henderson's brothel in Harlem in 1929 and turned to prostitution. The operation was raided. The police rounded up all the girls and arrested and booked them. Sadie lied under oath claiming 14-year-old Eleanora was an adult to prevent her from being sent to another home for wayward Black girls. The arrest records listed Eleanora as age 21. She served 100 days at Welfare Island, a workhouse. Then, she was released.

When Eleanora was 15 years old, Sadie was the housekeeper at Clara Winston's place. Eleanora helped Sadie work, but when she could, she sneaked and poured herself a drink of gin. *Gin will make you sin*. When Eleanora heard the Fletcher Henderson band was playing in New York, she went to the set and waited to speak to her father Clarence who was the rhythm guitarist with the band from 1928 to 1933.

The members of the Fletcher Henderson Band were the first Negroes to play at the Roseland Ballroom. Eleanora heard her father was there; so, she waited on him in the hallway. As he walked in her sight, she said, "Hey daddy." He was unsettled that she called him daddy because he didn't want anyone, maybe the ladies, to know he was old enough to have a teenage daughter. He told Eleanora to call him anything but daddy. She retorted, "I'm going to call you daddy all night unless you give me some darn money for the rent[12]."

The threat worked. She got the money and took it home to Sadie so she could pay the rent. Clarence softened his encounters with Eleanora. Other encounters were more cordial. Clarence never denied his firstborn child. By the time father and daughter connected in a meaningful way, Eleanora was finding some semblance of financial independence. He was an instrumentalist who also had vocal skills. Clarence's first and rare vocal recording *My Kinda' Love* was recorded on March 13, 1929, with the Fletcher Henderson Band. Clarence noticed Eleanora's vocal gifts. He took Eleanora to the Rhythm Club, the Band Box and other places and introduced her to people he knew in the jazz scene.

The following year, 1930, Sadie and Eleanora were listed in the census as boarders in a Manhattan household. They were more than likely house cleaners. Eleanora complained to her friends because she hated maid work. Wages were low and the work was demeaning. But being a housekeeper was better than being a sex worker and going to jail. Eleanora did not want to be sent to another institution for Black youth where basic freedoms were restricted, and indignities were liberal.

The Great Depression sank in. Jobs were hard to come by. People were starving and begging for food and standing in soup lines. As the saying goes, *When White America catches a cold, Black America catches the flu*. In those days, there were no food stamps, HUD vouchers, or social programs for poor people. Sadie and Eleanora along with the rest of the western world suffered through tough times.

Sadie cleaned homes and cooked to earn money. Eleanora followed suit. Their work and living arrangements changed frequently. Eventually, the two moved back to Harlem to an apartment on 139th Street. Mother and daughter suffered through one winter without heat. Eleanora tried to obtain a job in a club as a dancer but was not good at it. She kept trying. She wanted a dignified job.

Sadie guarded their reputation and tried to keep their lives decent and in order. Later that year, Eleanora and her neighbor Kenneth Hollon, a tenor saxophone player, teamed up and performed at clubs for tips. Once she got her foot in the door, she was good; she worked regularly. She was even featured in a floor show with tap dancer Charles "Honi" Coles and bassist George "Pops" Foster.

Photograph of Bill Robinson a male, African American tap dancer, actor and, singer. 01.25.1933 Library of Congress

Honi made his debut professionally at the Lafayette Theater as a member of The Three Millers. He appeared in two movies in the 1980s *The Cotton Club* and *Dirty Dancing*. Pops was the oldest, age 38, of the trio. He was known for his slap bass playing on the string bass. Pops, a native of southern Louisiana, moved to New York in 1929. Pops played professionally with the King Oliver Band and Louis Armstrong. King Oliver was a jazz legend from New Orleans and Louis Armstrong's mentor. Kenneth Hollon had a long run with Eleanora. He played in Billie Holiday and her Orchestra well into the 1950s. The great tap dancer Bill "Bojangles" Robinson, was an international attraction at the Lafayette Theater.

Eleanora bypassed the Cotton Club at the corner of 142nd Street and Lenox Avenue and sang primarily at small speakeasies. Originally the Cotton Club was Club Deluxe, a 400-seat nightclub owned by Heavyweight Boxing Champion Jack Johnson. He opened Club Deluxe in 1920. But his taste for white women became a problem to the White establishment. That year he had to serve time for driving his White fiancé or girlfriend over a state line which authorities claimed violated a federal law – The Mann Act which was enacted to prohibit the "White Slave" prostitution trade. Jack Johnson was prosecuted, tried, and sentenced to serve one year and one day under the law for driving a white woman across state lines for immoral purposes.

Jack Johnson was famous, flamboyant, and he openly dated white women. He married two white women. The white power structure punished him for breaking the unwritten interracial relationship code. The champ's imprisonment was an opportunity for mobsters to obtain a prime piece of property. Public policies are enforced to bankrupt successful Black people. Jack Johnson was forced to go to prison on trumped up charges.

Billie Holiday: Jazz Singer

Jack Johnson and his wife Etta, full-length portrait, standing, wearing winter coats, 1910. By Elmer Chickering. Library of Congress

In 1922, Mobster Owney Madden became the new manager and co-owner of Club Deluxe which was renamed the Cotton Club. Owney and his gangster business partners transformed the décor into a southern plantation theme and increased the seating to 700. Then, a chorus line was added; the club featured weekly radio broadcasts. The Cotton Club became the most popular club in Harlem. Like the business owners in Storyville, the Italian business owners hired the best Negro entertainment, but they did not give a flip about the rights of the Negro entertainers, who could not use the restroom where they worked or sit in the audience to enjoy the entertainment.

Fancy cars owned by flamboyant gangsters, movie stars, and business moguls parked in front of the Cotton Club. There was entertainment in thousands of speakeasies in New York City and on Jungle Alley and on Swing Street. Eleanora and her friends walked toward the lights. Artie Shaw, age 20, recalled club hopping one night in Harlem and hearing Eleanora sing in 1930. As Artie and Eleanora became more acquainted, he discovered he was five years her senior. Therefore, the night in 1930 that Artie was introduced to the improvising voice of Eleanora in a small place which could barely house 50 guests, she was 15. He was impressed with her singing style.

Artie walked up to Eleanora and declared, "One day I'm going to have a band, and you're going to sing in it."

And Elenora replied, "Yeah, that'll be the day[13]."

At that moment Artie, the son of two Jewish immigrants, was dreaming of his future success. On the other hand, Eleanora was trying to eat and trying to help her mother pay the rent. She had no concept of stardom in her future.

In 1930, Black – White race matters were so toxic that it was inconceivable to Eleanora to imagine a Black female singing in a band led by a white musician. Artie Shaw was trying to find a bright spot in the world of jazz; he spotted Eleanora and he saw a spark in her singing ability, and he teasingly promised her he was going to make a place in the music world and invite her in it. His dream came true. By the end of the decade, he was a big bandleader.

In 1931, Eleanora, age 16, met Bobby Henderson at Basement Brownies, an after-hour joint downstairs on West 133rd Street, a place popular with swing music, in Jungle Alley. The featured artist Eleanora, who was 5'8' weighed 200 pounds, was not dressing like a star, but she was singing like one. The piano player, Dot Hill, knew Bobby was a pianist and invited Bobby to play. Bobby played the cords to *Sweet Sue*.

Eleanora listened to Bobby play and studied his musical style. People in the audience requested the duo perform several songs. She was a natural entertainer. Eleanora and Bobby flirted with each other while he played the piano, and she sang and the two exchanged one-liners. Bobby said Eleanora listened to him play *Sweet Sue* before she sang a tone. She was great. They became a team. He became her regular pianist. Then, Eleanora and Bobby became lovers and inseparable.

Eleanora was a singer with ears. All great singers have good ears. Eleanora obtained her musical training in Baltimore, but she was honing her talents in Harlem. Eleanora and Bobby teamed up for gigs at other establishments including Pod's and Jerry's Log Cabin on 168 West and 133rd Street. Eleanora planned to audition to dance at Pod's and Jerry's, known for great fried chicken and piano playing. She admitted to the pianist that she could sing. He told her to give him a song. *"Trav'llin All Alone,"* she replied. She sang so emotionally, the customers started putting their drinks down. She had her own sound. She was intimate with the audience who felt she was singing to them. By the time she sang, *Body and Soul*, the audience was in tears.

Eleanora, who had not become Billie Holiday yet, was listening to the pianist as if she were a sophisticated instrumentalist. Bobby remembered that Eleanora was unique. Other girl singers at the time imitated Ethel Waters, a Cotton Club star. Ethel started singing in Baltimore, Maryland in the Black vaudeville circuit. She worked in Atlanta clubs with Bessie Smith where she sang ballads leaving the blues tunes for Bessie. Ethel moved to Harlem in the 1920s. Pianist Fletcher Henderson accompanied her. In the early 1930s, *Stormy Weather* became her featured song. Duke Ellington directed the house band.

The teen duo Bobby and Eleanora connected with other musicians, and they worked at other spots including Monette's, owned by the blues singer Monette Moore, whose records, labeled race music, were originally recorded under the name Susie Smith in 1923. Commercially, the recordings of Black people were classified as race music and race records until the 1940s when the Rhythm and Blues genre emerged.

Although Eleanora was young, she had a unique singing style. Eleanora was not trying to imitate the sound of any other singer. When she lived in Black Baltimore, she and her family were -scrubbing and bleaching dirty steps white- poor. She admired the people she saw in the night life scene who were well to do sporting pretty dresses and wearing fancy hats and popping dollars. She admired the well to do – whether they were legitimate or not. In the red-light or pleasure district, fine dressing was status. Eleanora admired the participants of the nightlife and indulged in it all – music, musical battles, sex, reefer, and whiskey.

When Eleanora joined Sadie in New York, Sadie had not discovered a path out of poverty. She went for what she knew. She knew how to cook and clean. At night there were bright lights in the entertainment district. Eleanora teamed up with other teens seeking to get their feet in the door of the entertainment world – a leg up for them in this journey called life. Entertainment presented possibilities more desirable than cleaning for white folks, where one was underpaid, slept in cold basements or bloom closets.

In 1931, at age 16, Eleanora combined her nickname Bill with Billie Dove her favorite actor and took her father's surname and she gave herself the stage name 'Billie Holiday.' At some point the spelling of her father's surname changed from Halliday to Holiday. By then, Billie had the opportunity to connect with her father Clarence when he performed in New York. Sometimes Eleanora was introduced as the daughter of Clarence Holiday who was a well-known jazz guitarist with the Fletcher Henderson Band. Billie Holiday considered her father's lifestyle as superior to her mother's image and lifestyle. Some children adore absent parents. Billie was simply thrilled to be in her father's company and in his favor.

Billie and her musician friends were grateful to earn tips in Harlem, a place bustling with entertainment where alcohol was sold all night. Harlem also contained 'hooch joints' inside apartments which were full of entertainment. Billie Holiday recalled in an interview that she earned $14 per week in tips when she became a regular singer in the jazz clubs in Harlem toward the end of Prohibition (1920 - 1933).

Ralph Cooper, the emcee at the Apollo Theatre in Harlem, NY said of hearing Billie Holiday sing, "It ain't the blues. I don't know what it is, but you got to hear it.[14]" In her own words Billie said, "I got my manner from Bessie Smith and Louis Armstrong, honey. Wanted her feeling and Louis' style.[15]"

Harlem was wide open 24/7. Near the corner of Lenox Avenue and 131st Street, the 'reefer man' sold two marijuana cigarettes for 25¢[16]. Street vendors including the peanut man and food vendors worked late. The Radium Club on Lenox and 142nd Street had a Sunday breakfast dance at 4am. Club Hot-Cha opened at 2am. Tillie's on 133rd Street offered great finger licking fried chicken. Visitors could catch a show at the Lafayette Theatre on Fridays featuring Bill 'Bojangles' Robinson, the world's greatest tap dancer. One had to be good on any stage in a club in Harlem, and good talent was everywhere on every corner along the entertainment strips.

By age 17, Billie Holiday was playing at Covan's (known later as Monette's) at 148 West 133rd Street in Harlem. Though she had an exceptionally low voice range, Billie Holiday was the undisputed greatest jazz singer. Her style of singing was spontaneous. Jazz musicians improvised and played music on the spot which requires a lot of musical skill. Jazz differed from classical music. Jazz is drawn from individual musical expressions. Whereas classical music is formal music compositions where the conductor and the musician's read music and play instruments producing a controlled sound.

Billie Holiday: Jazz Singer

In 1932, Billie was able to meet her father at Big John's Café on Seventh Avenue in Jungle Alley. Trombonist J.C. Higginbotham of the Fletcher Henderson band remembered Billie's solos standing out at Big Johns. Benny Carter, a musician and the music arranger for the Fletcher Henderson Band, said of Billie's vocals around age 17, "I felt that she had a touch of greatness in her.[17]"

The Prohibition act was repealed in 1933. Speakeasy businesses thrived. The word, speakeasy, was British slang, meaning 'smuggler's house' where illegal whiskey was sold. Mobsters heading organized crime gangs created lucrative businesses during prohibition. Al Capone earned $60 million a year supplying illegal beer and whiskey to thousands of speakeasies each year in the 1920s. New York gangsters Lucky Luciano, Salvatore Maranzano, Meyer Lansky, and Frank Costello controlled the profits of 32,000 speakeasies across New York[18].

John Hammond frequented the club circuit; but he did not drink alcohol or smoke reefer. His interest was signing new talent in the music industry and distributing records in the jukebox industry. Hammond was born into wealth. He was the oldest son of Emily Vanderbilt with John Henry Hammond and the grandson of William Henry Vanderbilt, who ran the Staten Island Railway. William became the richest American citizen in 1877 when he assumed responsibility for his father, Commodore Cornelius Vanderbilt's business assets which valued $100 million.

John Hammond, a well-known music columnist, wrote a column featuring Billie Holiday. He was quoted in *Melody Maker* saying that Billie Holiday was "a real find." He dubbed her, "incredibly beautiful and sings as well as anybody I ever heard[19]."

Hammond wrote, "Discovered a great singer, Billie Holiday, 200 pounds, beautiful, sings well.[20]" When Hammond first saw Billie Holiday singing at Monette Moore's place in Harlem, Billie was walking from table to table singing without a microphone.

Hammond was so impressed with Billie Holiday that he brought influential musicians and managers to Covan's to hear Billie Holiday sing. Billie Holiday was a musical genius. She used her emotions to interpret song lyrics. Her lyrical phrasing was sometimes akin to speech. Her voice was distinct; she sounded like her idol Louis Armstrong's horn.

One night, Monette invited John Hammond to her club so he could hear her sing, hoping he would sign her to a record label. Instead of him signing Monette, he offered to record Billie Holiday. Monette was furious that her opportunity landed in the lap of an unknown, unrecorded teenager. Hammond referred to Billie Holiday as "a real find" because she had emerged as a jazz singer with a new sound. Monette was defeated by the turn of events, and she left New York and relocated her establishment to Los Angeles, California. Monette later recorded *Rhythm for Sale* and *Two Old Maids in a Folding Chair* in 1936 and *Another Woman's Man* and *Please Mr. Blues* in 1947 through Decca Records.

Billie Holiday's singing career launched because she offered a new sound. She accepted her opportunity. Then, she started singing at the Log Cabin at 168 133rd Street. In those days, girl singers lifted their dresses to pick up dollar bill tips between their thighs. Women were sexualized in the workplace especially the entertainment industry. Billie grew tired of accepting so little for so much and stopped adhering to the demeaning practice. Fellow entertainers considered Billie's gesture ladylike. She was a class act. Male patrons including John Hammond handed dollar bills directly to Billie Holiday.

The lyrics she sang are as follows:

Would ja' for a big red apple?
Would ja' for my peace of mind?
Could ja' for a big red apple?
Give me what I'm trying to find?[21]

John Hammond set up Billie Holiday's first recording. When Billie walked into the recording studio and saw the microphone she was overcome with fear. Buck (Ford L. "Buck" Washington) who performed in the Buck and Bubbles variety duo saw Billie was frightened and he consoled her. "Don't let all those white folks see you scared," he pleaded[22]. Buck was the pianist and Shirley Clay was on trumpet for the recording session.

Buck dared Billie to walk to the microphone. She eased over to the microphone and did her thing. After that, she owned every microphone she ran across. John William Sublett's stage name was Bubbles. Buck and Bubbles, who moved to Manhattan in 1919, were the first Black entertainers to perform at Radio City Music Hall and to appear on television. Radio City at 1260 6th Avenue in midtown Manhattan is the largest indoor theatre in the world. King Kong and over 700 movies were filmed there.

Benny Goodman was a White bandleader who was later labeled the "King of Swing" until the mid-1940s. The band and Billie Holiday recorded *Your Mother's Son-In-Law* and

Riffin the Scotch. By the end of 1933 and into 1934 *Riffin the Scotch* reached number 6 on the pop charts. John Hammond wrote in his music column, "She was the first girl singer I'd come across who actually sang like an improvising jazz genius.[23]"

Billie Holiday earned $35 for her first recording session. In 1933, artists did not earn royalties. When her records started selling, Billie went to the label and asked for more money. Bernie Hanighen negotiated with Columbia Record label executives to pay Billie an additional $75 and for the label to add the name 'Billie' to the songs rather than the word 'vocalist.'

The Apollo Theatre, which seated 1,500 people opened its doors at 253 West 125th Street in Harlem between Seventh Avenue and Eighth Avenue to Black entertainers and audiences on January 26, 1934, giving birth to the long-standing Wednesday night weekly talent show. Club owners often shared their views about new talent. Frank Schiffman, who ran the LaFayette Theatre and the Apollo, praised Billie Holiday as a talented singer. Frank told Ralph Cooper who ran the Hotcha Club, "You never heard singing so slow, so lazy with such a drawl.[24]"

Billie Holiday was pleased with the raving reviews of her singing style. Though Holiday's range was low, she sang directly into the mic to make sure audiences heard her. Holiday mastered making a few notes count. Billie Holiday inspired her listeners. She quickly became a local sensation. As her local notoriety grew, poets penned poems about her. That year, 18-year-old Billie Holiday made her first appearance at the Apollo as an established singer. Frank Schiffman hired Billie Holiday to be a featured singer at the Apollo at $50 per week for two

Billie Holiday: Jazz Singer

weeks. Pianist Bobby Henderson accompanied her.

Shortly after Billie's Apollo Theater debut, she and Bobby broke up. He was so broken-hearted that he went into seclusion. The cause of the breakup is not known. However, John Hammond recalled that after Billie recorded *Riffin' the Scotch* with Benny Goodman, the two had a one-night stand. Billie became close friends with 24-year-old Tenor Saxophonist Lester Young during this time. At age 18, Billie was free spirited. Bobby, age 24, was more settled. Buck Clayton, who met Billie Holiday when she was 18, recalled, "By the time I met her she was country-looking but city slick[25]." In those days, her hair was short and curly. Billie wore flannel dresses which hung below her knees and two-tone flat Oxford shoes.

Riffin' the Scotch lyrics:

I jumped out of the frying pan
and right into the fire
When I lost me a cheating man
and got a no-count liar
Swipe the old for the new one
And now the new one's breaking my heart
I jumped out of the frying pan
and right into the fire
Lord, right into the fire[26]

Billie never competed in amateur competitions at the Apollo. By 1934, she was a popular artist in Harlem. Photographs show Billie Holiday autographing programs and papers for fans outside of the Apollo. John Hammond signed Billie Holiday to Brunswick Records that year. She recorded pop tunes with the Teddy Wilson band. The songs were converted to the swing genre so Hammond could sell the records in the jukebox market.

Ben Webster, Billie Holiday & Johnny Russell, Harlem, 1935
Name of guitarist and man in front of Billie is unknown.
Courtesy JP Redfern's Jazz Archive.

Lester Young performed at the Apollo that year too. He and Billie Holiday met at a jam session and became friends instantly. Her bond with Lester was so strong that she invited him to live in her mother Sadie's apartment instead of with the Henderson family. Lester recalled later that Billie showed him around Harlem and took him to various nightspots which were full of jazz and helped him get some gigs. He rejoined the Fletcher Henderson band in New York in March of 1934 before the band left to tour in Europe. Lester nicknamed Billie Holiday, Lady Day and Sadie, the Duchess. Billie named him Prez - as in

President of the saxophone players.

According to Biographer Douglas Daniels, Author, *Lester Leaps In: The Life and Times of Lester Young*. Lester Young's *Blue Devils* bandmates disputed Billie Holiday's claim that she nicknamed Lester Young, "Prez." The bandmates reported that they started calling Lester 'Prez' in 1932-1933. In other words, Lester's former bandmates claimed Billie started calling Lester 'Prez' when he nicknamed her 'Lady Day' and her mother Sadie 'Duchess' in 1934 while he lived in their apartment briefly. However, by his own admission, Lester Young told Chris Albertson in an interview at WCAU-FM radio in Philadelphia, Pennsylvania on August 24, 1958, that Billie Holiday nicknamed him Prez.

Chris Albertson asked Lester Young, "When did you first meet Billie Holiday?"

"When I came to New York in 1934," Lester replied.

Lester added, "I used to live at her house with her mother you know, 'because I didn't know my way around. She taught me a lot of things, you know. She got me little record dates, you know. Play behind her and solos…"

"Well, you're her favorite soloist," Chris declared.

"She is mine," Lester replied lovingly with warm laughter.

"It's a drone," Lester added.

"I understand she gave you the name Prez. Didn't she?" Chris reported.

"Yes, she did. And I gave her the name of Lady Day[27]," Lester agreed.

Billie Holiday teamed up with Teddy Wilson, a native of Austin Texas, who studied the piano and the violin at Tuskegee Institute in Tuskegee, Alabama. He previously played for Speed Webb, Louis Armstrong, and Earl Hines. Teddy joined the Benny Goodman Trio two years after Billie Holiday recorded her first singles becoming the first Black musician to play in an integrated jazz band. Teddy was three years older than Billie Holiday; musically the pair had amazing chemistry. Brunswick Records recorded Teddy playing piano for Billie Holiday, Lena Horne, and Helen Ward. He also recorded with Lester Young, Roy Eldridge, Buck Clayton, and Ben Webster.

Ella Fitzgerald, age 17, appeared at the Apollo to compete for amateur night that year. Like Billie Holiday, Ella originally planned to try her hand as an entertainer at dancing but changed courses at the last minute and sang a tune. Ella made the right move; she won first place. She too stood in line to get Billie Holiday's signature. They became fast friends. Like Billie, Ella put a stamp on the jazz genre as a scat singer. In 1935, Ella became the featured singer of the Chick Webb Orchestra. Then, she, age 18, recorded her first jazz record *Love and Kisses*.

In 1935, two years after her first recording, Billie Holiday, age 20, appeared in Duke Ellington's short nine-minute film *Symphony in Black: A Rhapsody of Negro Life* where she starred alongside Duke Ellington. The film highlighted Ellington's musical piece *A Rhapsody of Negro Life.* Duke Ellington knew Clarence Holiday. Over the years, the two played in the same venues. *Symphony in Black* won an Academy Award for best musical short subject. Naturally,

Billie's role in the film introduced her to a larger audience beyond New York's legendary jazz world.

Duke Ellington, Howard Theater, 1938. Library of Congress

Billie Holiday recorded *The Saddest Tale* with the Duke Ellington Orchestra in *Symphony in Black: A Rhapsody of Negro Life*. The song was suggestive of the role Billie played of a woman being abused by her lover. The short film produced by Paramount Pictures and distributed by Paramount Pictures was 9 minutes and 41 seconds.

The Saddest Tale lyrics:

> *The saddest tale told on land and sea.*
> *Is the tale told when they told the truth on me.*
>
> *The saddest tale told on land and sea.*
> *Is the tale told when they told the truth on me*[28].

Duke Ellington was a jazz giant. He was a brilliant pianist, songwriter, and composer. The decade *Symphony in Black* was filmed, Duke Ellington and his band occupied two railroad cars when they toured the country. Other bands travelled in buses. Duke Ellington carried the most elite and well-paid musicians in the nation. His compositions were in the league with Bach, a famous 17th century German classical music composer. Jazz critics never gave him his due credit as a composer. Duke Ellington's Orchestra played 52 weeks each year. Duke Ellington was in demand night after night and week after week. His band survived the Great Depression, never downsized, and kept going throughout his life.

In 1935, Billie Holiday recorded several singles: *What a Little Moonlight Can Do*, *Miss Brown to You,* and *A Sunbonnet Blue and A Yellow Straw Hat*. Billie Holiday's career blossomed as she recorded hit after hit with pianist and composer Teddy Wilson. *Symphony in Black* was the only film in 1935 starring a Black cast. *The Littlest Rebel* (1 hour, 13 minutes) featuring Shirley Temple, child star and Bojangles, famous Negro tap dancer and actor, previewed that year. *The Littlest Rebel* highlighted American racial entertainment norms. One of Temple's lines in the movie was *"I'm a Confederate."* Bill "Bojangles" Robinson played the role of a butler on a southern plantation. There were no strong "Black Panther" characters in Hollywood then. Black actors were relegated to subservient characters such as house cleaners and butlers.

Bessie Smith recorded her last four records: *Do Your Duty*, *Gimme a Pigfoot*, *Take me for a Buggy Ride*.. November 24, 1933, in Columbia studios 72 hours after Billie Holiday recorded her first records in the same studio. Bessie was paid $50 per record which was less than she earned in her heyday when she earned $2,000 per concert. Bessie was reinventing her sound from her regular blues tunes to fit into the Swing era. Her stage presence was loud. Audiences loved her. Bessie was a high earning vaudeville performer. Vaudeville acts slowed down during the Great Depression. Unfortunately, income derived from Vaudeville shows slowed down too.

John Hammond invited Bessie Smith to New York to record for Okeh Records, an imprint for race records owned by Columbia Records. Columbia first recorded Bessie Smith in 1923. Bessie Smith and her five siblings started performing on street corners when they were children so they could buy bread, meat, and necessities after they parents died. Bessie started dancing professionally at age 18 with a group which included her older brother Clarence. Ma Rainey, known as the "Mother of the Blues," was the lead singer. After Bessie Smith developed a personal stage presence she went solo, and her popularity and income soared like the eagle.

On the other hand, Billie's recording, at age 18 launched a new era of jazz singing. Billie Holiday's stage presence was the opposite of her idol Bessie Smith. Billie didn't walk the stage and she was not loud. She was cool and elegant. Billie stood in one place singing, swaying softly, bending her right arm outward, and titling her head from left to right giving the audience direct eye contact. She often held her index finger and thumb close as if she were going to pop her fingers. Like her father, Billie started performing early. She started singing for small crowds at age 13.

New York, N.Y. Dancers at the Hurricane Ballroom dancing to the music of Duke Ellington and his Orchestra 1943. Photo by Gordon Parks

In the 1920s, when Billie Holiday was a little girl, Clarence Holiday, Duke Ellington, and others played in Baltimore at good time houses, dance halls, and private parties. People ate, drank, and danced at good time houses. Rooms were converted into hotel rooms as patrons could pay $1 to rent rooms for one hour for romantic escapades.

Billie Holiday: Jazz Singer

Duke Ellington, Junior Raglin, Tricky Sam Nanton, Juan Tizol, Barney Bigard, Ben Webster, Otto Toby Hardwick(e), Harry Carney, Rex William Stewart, and Sonny Greer, Howard Theater 1938, Washington, DC.

Coleman Hawkins, Clarence Holiday, Benny Goodman, and others stood on the shoulders of Fletcher Henderson, who worked at Black Swan Records which was the first Black owned recording company in the United States. In the early 1920s, he was the pianist on over 150 records at Swan Records until 1923. He played for Ethel Waters. He became a bandleader in 1923. Louis Armstrong played trumpet in the Fletcher Henderson band in 1924. Coleman Hawkins was the saxophonist in the Fletcher Henderson band from 1924-1934.

Coleman Hawkins popularized the tenor saxophone sound in New York jazz through the Fletcher Henderson Band. Before Coleman Hawkins, Louis Armstrong's trumpet solo style dominated jazz bands. Early jazz instrumentation included the trumpet, trombone, and clarinet. The rhythm section contained the guitar, banjo, string bass or tuba, piano and drums.

Flash Weekly Newspicture Magazine, 1937-1939

Billie Holiday: Jazz Singer

The flow of money slowed down during The Great Depression and Fletcher Henderson was not able to keep his band together. In 1934, Benny Goodman purchased 36 arrangements from Fletcher Henderson and Benny introduced more whites to jazz. For a while during the Depression, Fletcher's earnings were derived from composing music for Benny Goodman. Fletcher's arrangements became the standard for the swing sound.

Clarence Holiday didn't believe audiences would accept his daughter's singing style. Yet, he was positive about her chosen profession. Billie sounded like Louis Armstrong's horn rather than her predecessor Ethel Waters or her idol Bessie Smith. Ethel was the 5th Black female recording artist in the United States of America. Ethel recorded her first record in 1921 with Black Swan Records. She was the first Black woman to record an album at Cardinal Records.

Bessie's first record, *Crazy Blues*, recorded in 1920, sold over 100,000 copies. Three years later Bessie Smith moved to New York and was rejected by Black Swan Records because she was considered too rough. Black Swan's loss was Columbia Records gain. Columbia signed her and recorded *Downhearted Blues* which sold over 2 million copies. Bessie Smith became famous that year. Columbia Records executives were *popping bottles*.

W.E.B. DuBois, an intellectual who founded *Crisis* magazine, which provided financial support to Black Swan, felt Bessie Smith was unladylike. Yet, he and others were surprised at her commercial success. Columbia recorded 160 Bessie Smith tunes. She was accompanied by leading musicians of the time including Louis Armstrong, Coleman Hawkins, Fletcher Henderson, James P. Johnson, and Charlie Green. Dozens of her songs became bestselling records.

Benny Goodman 3rd and band Teddy Wilson seated

Billie Holiday's neighbor, Miles Davis, who became a jazz great, was a Coleman Hawkins fan and mentee. Early on, Miles was a sideman. He played trumpet on three Coleman Hawkins tunes for the *Hollywood Stampede* album. Like Bessie Smith, Louis Armstrong, Duke Ellington, Billie Holiday, Charlie Parker and others, Miles Davis was dedicated to his art form through constant practice and experimentation; self-discipline is required for one to master the art of playing an instrument.

Art gets better over time. As the adage goes, "Practice makes perfect." By age 20, Billie Holiday advanced from her days of earning tips to landing a role in a short film. Her art was earning her more money than many of her adult neighbors in Harlem who were earning $25 to $30 per week working low wage jobs. Frank Schiffman offered to put Billie Holiday on a bill at Club Hot-Cha. Billie earned

Billie Holiday: Jazz Singer

$50 per week singing at Club Hot-Cha, an after-hour club which obtained customers after 2am. Thanks to Billie's role in *Symphony in Black* her popularity widened, especially in her local base.

Mastery sets one apart from average. Miles admired Billie Holiday too. Miles said respectfully, "Billie Holiday didn't need any horns. She sounded like horns.[29]" Billie said herself, "I don't think I'm singing. I feel like I'm playing a horn.[30]"

David Margolick proposed that Billie Holiday was trying to sound like a horn and the horn players wanted to sound like a singer. Lester Young agreed. He said jazz instrumentalists wanted to sing lyrics through the chambers of their instruments.[31] Like great musicians, Billie Holiday's voice perfected the secret of great jazz – a music form unique from pop, blues, and classical.

Billie Holiday's idol Louis Armstrong, known as Pops, Satch, and Satchmo, was influenced by early jazz, which was prominent in Storyville, a redlight district in the French Quarters in New Orleans, his native city, which flourished from 1898 to 1917. During the district's peak, there were 40 bordellos and 2,000 prostitutes in the area. Elite prostitute services ranged from $5 per hour and up at a time when the average American worker earned 22¢ per hour. Reportedly, Pops' mother worked in a parlor briefly. The madam business operators and owners hired local musicians who had freedom of expression. Their sound, an outgrowth of Blues and Ragtime music, became known as jazz[32] Redlights districts were rife with music, pleasures, and opportunities.

Storyville was named for New Orleans Alderman Sidney

Story who successfully pushed the passage of an ordinance to end citywide prostitution by relegating brothels, saloons, and other entities to designated streets: Bienville, Conti, Customhouse, St. Louis, Marais, North Basin, North Franklin, North Robertson, Treme, and Villere streets in January of 1897. Other populated cities created redlight districts too. The fancy brothels on North Basin Street attracted famous guests like Babe Ruth.

Teddy Wilson and Zutty Singleton, Turkish Embassy, Washington, D.C., 1940. Library of Congress

The City of New Orleans closed Storyville, a Negro and Creole business strip in 1917 where brothel owners were immorally and sinfully rich beyond measure. King Oliver and his crew left New Orleans when entertainment money dried up and went to Chicago. Louis Armstrong left Chicago and went to New York.

Billie Holiday: Jazz Singer

Charlie Parker, Tommy Potter, Miles Davis, Duke Jordan, and Max Roach, Three Deuces, New York, N.Y., Aug. 1947

Many madams, all female, operated services from their establishments. Some services were operated from mansions. During slavery, some slave women were trafficked to the area. During WWI (1914-1918) military officials from a nearby Army base prompted the closure of Storyville proposing the environment had a negative impact on soldiers.

The negatives of the prostitution industry included passing sexually transmitted diseases. Syphilis was the worst infection. Syphilis if untreated causes severe problems including brain disorders and death. The disease can be transmitted from a mother to a child. The best cure for syphilis, penicillin, did not emerge until 1928. Penicillin was not distributed to Black communities until the late 1940s. People who participated in the Tuskegee

Experiment did not obtain penicillin until the 1960s.

New York created the Cabaret Licensing program which disproportionately created economic harm to Black jazz artists. The New York mobsters became so immorally and sinfully rich that they bought the police department, corrupted the judges, and initiated the War on Drugs.

Early in her career, Billie Holiday had a 10-year string of hits including *Twenty-Four Hours a Day*, *Summertime*, *The Way You Look Tonight*, *Carelessly*, and *Nice Work if You Can Get it*. *Carelessly* was a big hit. According to the 1937 Hits Archive, *Carelessly* featuring Billie Holiday on vocals and Teddy Wilson on piano was #1 on the weekly "Your Hit Parade" radio countdown.

Carelessly lyrics,

How carelessly you gave me your heart
And carelessly I broke it sweetheart
I took each tender kiss you gave me
Every kiss made you a slave to me[33]

Summertime lyrics,

Summertime
And the livin' is easy
Fish are jumpin'
And the cotton is high
Oh, your daddy's rich
And your ma is good lookin'
So hush, little baby
Don't you cry

One of these mornin's
You're goin' to rise up singin'

Billie Holiday: Jazz Singer

> Then you'll spread your wings
> And you'll take the sky
> But till that mornin'
> There's a-nothin' can harm you
> With daddy and mammy
> Standin' by[34]

In 1935, Benny Moten, the saxophonist in Count Basie's band died, and Lester Young replaced Benny. Lester's style shined like new money with his new bandmates. When Lester replaced Coleman Hawkins in the Fletcher Henderson band in 1934, his bandmates wanted Lester to imitate Coleman Hawkins's style. In the early 1930s, musicians idolized Coleman Hawkins and imitated his musical sound. Like Billie Holiday, Lester Young was determined to produce a new sound. Lester Young was one of Billie Holiday's influencers. Billie Holiday was initially part of Lester's social capital.

Count Basie built an all-star band with Saxophonist Lester Young, Trumpeter Roy Eldridge, and the Pianist Art Tatum. The instrumentalists in the Count Basie Band were forerunners to the bebop and the cool jazz genres. Billie Holiday and Lester Young created musical magic. Together sparks floated. Lester used to hold his saxophone up and out to the side blowing musical sounds in the air driving audiences wild.

Lester Young was born in Woodville, Wilkinson County, in Southwest Mississippi because his mother Lizetta wanted to give birth to her first child in her family home. However, Lester was raised 140 miles away in Algiers, Orleans Parish, Louisiana, on the West bank of the Mississippi river – five miles from New Orleans. He was six years older than Billie Holiday. His father Willis Lester Young, known affectionately as Billy, was a musician and the band leader of his family's vaudeville band called the Young Family Band which played a combination of ragtime and folk music. Lizetta played several instruments including the piano. At an early age, Lester learned to play the violin and the trumpet.

By age 10, in 1919, Lester learned to play the drums. His parents separated that year. His father obtained custody of the children; another version is that Willis's sister abducted the children when Lizetta left the children at home with her while she was running an errand. During the next eight years the family band expanded and toured with circuses, medicine shows, minstrels, parades, and carnivals from Pensacola, Florida to Seattle, Washington during summers and they toured in Minneapolis, Minnesota in the winter.

At age 12, Lester switched his instrument from the drums to the saxophone. Then, his three-year-old brother Lee started playing drums. Irma, age nine, played the alto saxophone. She too was musically talented. According to Biographer Douglas Daniels, Lester Young's birth name was Willis Lester Young Jr. He changed his name to Lester Willis Young. Lester left the family band in 1925 at age 16. He joined the Bostonians, a Kansas City band. Next, Lester joined King Oliver's Creole Jazz Band in New Orleans. Then, he joined the Oklahoma Blue Devils where he met Alto Saxophonist Buster Smith. Lester and Buster practiced for hours. Then, Lester developed a lighter tone. Lester was a virtuoso and king of the after hour all night jam contests in Kansas City. He played drums, the violin, the trumpet, and the tenor saxophone.

Lester was a lifelong friend of Billie Holiday. Band member Buck Clayton was also like a brother, though Billie and

Billie Holiday: Jazz Singer

Lester were remarkably close. Billie and Lester were so close onlookers assumed they were lovers. Lester grew up in his father's family band during the Vaudeville era. He discovered musical independence when he left the family band and played in other bands. Lester was one of the key innovators of the new jazz shift. In addition, his Lady Day was the first popular voice of a new jazz vocal sound.

JAZZ was influenced by African rhythms and European harmonic structure. African plantation field hollers, work songs, brass bands, funeral processions, parades, banjo performances, Negro spirituals, ragtime, and blues merged into jazz culture.

- **West African instruments:** Banjo, guitar and percussion
- **European instruments:** trumpet, trombone, saxophone, string bass, and piano
- **Early jazz instruments used:** cornet, clarinet, trombone, tuba or bass, piano, banjo and drums.

Jazz was cultivated in New Orleans between 1910 to 1915 in Storyville, the redlight district where wealthy brothel madams hired jazz musicians to perform live music in their mansion and palaces. Jazz was originally spelled '**Jass**,' slang for sex.

Storyville was closed in 1917. Then, King Oliver, Louis Armstrong and others left New Orleans and moved to Chicago, New York... Louis Armstrong popularized the swing genre. He taught Fletcher Henderson Band musicians including Coleman Hawkins how to swing.

Louis Armstrong stature, New Orleans
Photo by Carol P. Highsmith

Meredith Coleman McGee

Billie was wishing on a star. She had willpower. She tried. She tried. She tried. A small break came. Another break came. She gave her best and kept getting better. All right now. Get it girl!

Times Square, 1935-1945. Courtesy Library of Congress

Three

Columbia Years

The period from Billie Holiday's first recording at age 18 in 1933 to 1938, dubbed The First Period, are considered her finest years in jazz. Columbia Records was her first record label. Her complete works with Columbia include *The Quintessential Billie Holiday*, which is eight CDs or LPs and *Lady Day: A Collection of Classic Jazz Interpretations*. A few of her songs from this era, *Your Mother's Son-In-Law, Riffin' The Scotch, I Wished on the Moon, What a Little Moon Light Can Do, Miss Brown to You, Yesterdays, I Gotta' Right to Sing the Blues*... were performed in concert and in club settings, where she often captivated wealthy and professional white audiences, and in other settings her audience included Black people.

Columbia Records Talent Scout John Hammond discovered Billie Holiday in 1933 on Swing Street in Harlem at 148 W. 133rd Street, known now as Bill's Place. Hammond had a lengthy career. He launched and or reactivated the careers of a series of jazz, folk, R&B, and blues artists including Bessie Smith, Fletcher Henderson, Count Basie, Benny Goodman, Aretha Franklin, Bob Dylan, Bruce Springsteen, Robert Johnson, and Big Joe Turner... By 1934, Billie Holiday had covered the waterfront singing in jazz clubs in the Big Apple: The Yeah Man Club, Ubandi Club... Jazz musicians and sports writers coined the nickname 'Big Apple.'

Billie Holiday sang at Dickie Well's Clam House, where Dancer Detroit Red reported, she, Eleanora, and the other girls lifted their dresses and picked up their tips between their thighs. The club was also known for delicious Chicken and Waffles.

52nd Street, New York, N.Y., 1948 William P Gottlieb, Library of Congress

Detroit Red recalled in an interview with Linda Lipnack Huehl that people from all over the world visited Harlem for entertainment and a fun time. Detroit Red said the girls happily obtained big tips from rich white tourists, who usually went to the Cotton Club first then they trinkled to Harlem late night to the after-hour places. The girls were always eager to wait on wealthy whites who pulled up in limousines.

Billie Holiday's record label - Columbia Records is the

oldest surviving record label in the United States of America. The company goes back to the days when Americans used the gramophone and the phonograph - early record players. Columbia was involved in the evolution of records from brown wax records and black wax records to 78's, LP 33's, and 45s. Today, Columbia is one of four flagship record labels, RCA Records, Arista Records, and Epic Records, owned by Sony Music Entertainment which carries superstars like Jay-Z, Beyoncé, Céline Dion, Lady Gaga, Olivia Rodrigo, Calvin Harris, Marc Anthony, Pharrell Williams, Rihanna, Sean Love Combs, and Travis Scott.

According to Billie Holiday's stepmother, Fannie Holiday, Billie, and her father Clarence were on the same bill in Chicago in 1936. Clarence once asked his bandleader to consider allowing Billie to become the band's featured girl singer. The proposition never materialized but both Holidays (father and daughter) got the chance to perform in the same venue. Clarence was known for his ability to keep time for the band and helping the instrumentalists maintain their swinging tunes. Though Billie did not grow up under her father's thumb, she was influenced by the same musical district in Baltimore her father frequented when he started playing the banjo at age 14, in 1912, three years before her birth.

Clarence was proud of Billie. When he was in New York, he took her to spots such as the Rhythm Club, the Band Box, and Big John's Café in Jungle Alley. The Fletcher Henderson band often played at Big John's in the 1920s. Trombonist J.C. Higginbotham recalled that Billie Holiday was quiet and well-mannered around her father, and she sang when the opportunity presented itself.

Billie Holiday started recording at age 21 in 1936 with Tenor Saxophonist Lester Young. By then, her nickname "Lady Day" and Sadie's nickname "Duchess" were popular. Lester's nickname "Prez" stuck too. More people in the jazz world characterized him as the commander in chief saxophonist of jazz. Billie Holiday said of herself, Prez, her mother, and the Count Basie band, "We were the royal family[35]."

In 1936, Bernie Hanighen, assumed responsibility as producer for the Wilson-Holiday recording for Vocalion Records, a subsidiary of American Record Corporation which later merged with Columbia Records. Hanighen was a Harvard University graduate, who like John Hammond, spent his free time in Harlem listening to jazz. He doubled Billie Holiday's pay and added her name to the records as a leader. She always had the liberty of picking the songs she wanted to sing and the musicians she wanted to use. She recorded *No Regrets* on July 10, 1936. Artie Shaw played his clarinet and saxophone. Bunny Berigan, a trumpeter played alongside her for the recording.

No Regrets lyrics

No regrets
Although our love affair has gone astray
No regrets
I know I'll always care though you're away
So now our happy romance ended suddenly
Still in my heart you'll be forever mine [36]

She started touring with the Count Basie Orchestra in 1937. By then, she was obtaining top billings across the country. Billie communicated cozily with audiences. She assembled lyrics with symbolism which was characteristic of African speech.

Count Basie, Ray Bauduc, Bob Haggart, Harry Edison, Herschel Evans, Eddie Miller, Lester Young, Matty Matlock, June Richmond, and Bob Crosby, Howard Theater, Washington, D.C. 1941, Library of Congress

Jimmy Rushing was the band's blues singer. Billie Holiday left the blues tunes to Jimmy. She considered Jimmy Rushing one of her favorite blues singers. Billie was the only female in the band. She was one of the fellows when it came to smoking weed or shooting dice at the back of the bus.

She often sat next to Lester Young on the Count Basie bus when the band was touring. He was a positive force in her life. Billie had an affair with Rhythm Guitarist Freddie Green. Although Freddie was married, bandmates said Freddie treated Billie well. Reportedly, some of Freddie and Billie's quarrels were publicly displayed on the bus for all to hear or for bandmates to whisper about later.

Pianist Jimmie Rowles who accompanied Billie Holiday in the 1950s with Lester Young, recalled meeting Billie Holiday in 1942 when he was 20 years old. He said Billie was extremely comfortable in her nudeness. He noted that one night she called him to her dressing room doorway standing there naked in her heels and asked him to write out chords for a tune. He wrote the chords. He said, "She was something else! ...She was always happy when she knew Prez was playing for her. The way he played behind her. It was like she was in her mother's arms." He declared smiling, "Everyone loves a wild woman!"[37]

Like flies, male fans were attracted to Billie Holiday. Men often crowded around the bar where she was a patron or on the street waiting for her to walk outside so they could get Billie's autograph. She had star power and sex appeal. Bassist John Simmons said he admired Billie Holiday for a long time before she and he became lovers. He recalled that one night she walked out the door with a woman and the next night she chose him, and he was happy 'for the picking.' She was "a sex machine[38]," he declared. John said her conversational voice turned him on.

On Monday, March 1, 1937, Clarence Holiday, became extremely sick in Texas with his lung disorder. Some musicians in the Don Redman and His Orchestra drove Clarence to the closest hospital but he was refused service and by the time he made it to the VA's Colored ward in Dallas where he was finally able to obtain treatment, he had pneumonia and without antibiotics, Clarence died. The denial of healthcare was one of the gravest human right violations segregation policies posed against Black people.

The Germans introduced mustard gas in WWI to give them leverage over their enemies in the Allied powers: United States, Great Britain (UK), Italy, Russia, France, and Japan. Mustard gas blisters the skin, eyes, and lungs. During WWI, 120,000 soldiers exposed to mustard gas died. Billie Holiday was devastated when she lost her father at age 38. Billie connected to her father beautifully through music. After losing her father, Billie maintained a meaningful bond with her stepmother Fannie.

Clarence Holiday was buried in Brooklyn, New York in Cypress Hills National Cemetery which was reserved for members of the Armed Forces. He was a jazz musician in a world where fame did not necessarily breed fortune and where racism and discrimination made life a 'bitch.' The loss of her father truly left a hole in Billie's heart. The stench of racism and her loss was piercing deep.

Six months later in September of 1937, Billie's musical idol, Bessie Smith died from injuries she sustained in a car accident on Highway 61 in Mississippi near Clarksdale and the crossroad where the legend of Bluesman Robert Johnson selling his soul to the devil to obtain electrifying guitar skills was born. Bessie Smith was 43 years old. She was in the process of making another musical comeback. She had a mega fan base. Reportedly, 7,000 people attended her funeral at O.V. Catto Elks Lodge. Over 30,000 people viewed her body while it lay in state. Fans pushed and shoved their way inside the church to pay their respects to the Empress of the Blues. Flowers arrived from across the globe. Her body was laid to rest at Mount Lawn Cemetery in Philadelphia, Pennsylvania.

Billie Holiday grieved. She lost her father after developing a meaningful relationship with him from age 13 to age 22. Then, she lost her idol Bessie Smith which was like losing a close cousin. But Billie stayed busy singing, touring, and recording. She was in demand. Billie Holiday put her pain into her music.

The Devil's Crossroads sign in Clarksdale, a prominent home to old-time blues music in the Mississippi (River) Delta region in Northwest Mississippi by Carol H. Highsmith, Library of Congress

Billie learned how *to play with and against* the jazz mode in Baltimore. She learned how to improve dull melodies. Whitley Balliett proclaimed that Billie pronounced words with clarity and caricature turning songs completely around. She used her voice as a horn to strengthen lyrics. In 1937, Billie Holiday and Saxophonist Lester Young turned around *Me, Myself, and I*[39] Buck Clayton was on

Billie Holiday: Jazz Singer

trumpet. Other musicians included Edmond Hall, clarinet; Lester Young, tenor saxophone; James Sherman, piano; Walter Page, bass; Freddie Green, guitar; and Jo Jones, drums. Vocalion Records recorded *Me, Myself, and I* on a 78, June 15, 1937. The record was the company's first recording.

Me, Myself, and I song lyrics:

Me, myself, and I
Are all in love with you
We all think you're wonderful, we do
Me, myself, and I
Have just one point of view
We're convinced there's no one else like you

It can't be denied, dear
You brought the sun to us
We'd be satisfied, dear
If you'd belong to one of us

So, if you pass me by
Three hearts will break in two
'Cause me, myself, and I
Are all in love with you[40]

In August of 1938, Billie Holiday and Boogie-Woogie Pianist Big Joe Turner, a Kansas City, Missouri native, appeared on the same bill for a week at the Apollo Theater. Boggie-Woogie was a contemporary dance craze which Turner and other pianists: Albert Ammons, Pete Johnson, and Lux Lewis introduced to New Yorkers.

Big Joe Turner was a blues shouter. His popular song in the 1930s was *Rock the Joint Boogie*. He later became

65

famously known in 1954 for his hit song *Shake, Rattle, and Roll*. He is the Father of Rock and Roll. In 1938, Billie Holiday, age 23, added *This Year's Kisses* and *Mean to Me* to her song list.

Eventually Billie Holiday's tenure with the Count Basie Orchestra ended. Count Basie Band member Jo Jones determined that Billie Holiday was fired from the Basie Band by John Hammond because she refused to sing the blues. On at least one occasion, Billie declared that it was she who turned in her resignation letter because Count Basie had too many bosses over his band.

Jo Jones announced his view on John Hammond, "He wanted her to be a colored mammy[41]." Jo Jones added, "We were going through hell." There is truth to both versions of the story. White professionals normalized Black stereotypes. Jazz artists were jumping out of the boxes which White America determined Black Americans fit neatly in. When Lester Young was a teenager, he refused to continue to travel through the south with the family band because racism was constant and demeaning. Billie Holiday preferred to sing jazz and pop tunes. As artists Billie and Lester believed they owned creative liberties. John Hammond denied firing Billie. His version of the matter was that Billie quit. She publicly agreed.

Jo Jones related to the troubled life of his race. At times, jazz musicians lived on earth in hell. Yet, they created, improvised, and set themselves apart as often as possible. Jo Jones and Lester Young were playing a gig in Los Angeles when an army man in the audience dressed in a Zoot suit caught up with Jo and Lester who had avoided the WWII draft. However, the military was much softer on white jazz musicians than they were on Jo and Lester.

Billie Holiday: Jazz Singer

Glenn Miller and Artie Shaw were placed in band outfits during their military tour. Lester Young and Jo Jones were not allowed to play their instruments. Lester was relegated to manual and hard labor.

As Jo Jones knew personally, Billie Holiday did not like domestic work, and she did not want to portray the image of a mammy or a maid in film. However, she played a maid in her second film but at least she was able to sing in her role. It would have been that role or nothing at all. Publicly, Billie was flashy like the boys she admired in Baltimore. She sported jewels and diamonds and dressed in minks and furs; her hair was always styled. She earned money as a singer and spent it all on her image and pleasures.

Black musicians and singers endured a lot travelling in America. There was nothing fun about going in the woods to relieve one's bowels, or using the service elevator, or walking through the kitchen or back door to get to the stage to entertain white audiences or being called a 'nigger' or a 'boy' or a 'nigger wench.' Billie Holiday was once forced to apply dark makeup in Detroit before a performance to ensure that the white audience did not confuse her racial identity as white since she was fair skinned with long naturally silky hair. Whether Billie was fired, or she quit, her tenure as the featured singer for the Count Basie Orchestra ended.

However, Billie Holiday continued to perform and record with members of Count Basie's band. On January 16, 1938, the third Sunday in the month, Bennie Goodman played a famous jazz concert in Carnegie Hall featuring a racially mixed orchestra which included key jazz musicians from the swing era: Lester Young, on saxophone, Buck Clayton, on trumpet, and Count Basie and Teddy Wilson on piano. That evening, the Savoy Ballroom, which was owned by two Jewish businessmen, Jay Faggen and Moe Gale and managed by Charles Buchanan a native of the West Indies, sponsored a battle of the bands featuring the establishment's house band the Chick Webb Band whose singer was Ella Fitzgerald against the Count Basie Band with Billie Holiday on vocals.

Ella Fitzgerald, Dizzy Gillespie, Ray Brown, Milt (Milton) Jackson, and Timmie Rosenkrantz, Downbeat, New York, N.Y. Sept. 1947. Library of Congress

The *New York Amsterdam News* reported that Ella, age 21, went to the mic wearing white fighting togs. Billie, age 23, wore pink during the entire battle. Ella sang *Loch Lomond* and Billie sang *My Man*. When the ballots were tallied, Chick Webb and Ella won the battle three to one. The Basie Band had a bluesy sound, while Chick Webb's band had an Eastern influence. Chick Webb, a Baltimorean, was a drummer and a band leader. Chick was short in statute 4'1" tall but he was a giant when it came to music and conducting music. Both Billie and Ella had different and unique voice attributes.

Eyewitnesses felt Count Basie and Billie Holiday won. But make no mistake about it, Ella Fitzgerald, who had broken out of an institution for wayward Black girls, was homeless at age 14, and won first place at the Apollo Theater at age 17, was a jazz star in 1938. Billie Holiday and Ella Fitzgerald mutually respected each other whether it was raining, sleeting, or snowing.

In 1938, 21-year-old Ella Fitzgerald released her first hit *A-Tisket, A-Tasket* which she co-wrote while she was the female singer for the Chick Webb Orchestra. Like Louis Armstrong, Ella was an expert jazz scat singer. She too was the only female in an all-male band. The Chick Webb band often battled other bands. Win or lose there was no bad blood among jazz band members. Jazz musicians honored sportsmanship rules. Fighting racism was enough.

Billie Holiday, at age 23, became the featured singer with the Artie Shaw Orchestra becoming the first Black female attraction to tour with a white orchestra. By then, in addition to being a clarinetist, Artie Shaw was a composer. Artie planned for Billie Holiday to tour with his band containing 14 white men as a star because he viewed her as the best jazz singer on the scene. He planned for Billie's star power to help lift the status of his band. He told her when she was 15 years old that she would be in his band. Who would have known in 1930 that his vision would materialize? It did. However, Jazz critics opposed Artie Shaw's vocal choice. *DownBeat* ran a negative editorial about Artie Shaw adding Billie Holiday as a star to his band. Nasty rumors spread and song publishers wanted Shaw to drop Billie. He refused to concede.

He stuck to his guns and decided to tour through the south with Billie Holiday regardless of the negative press. Promoters objected to Billie Holiday being on bills simply because she was Black. Had Artie Shaw chosen a white singer the white press would have written positive reviews. Artie Shaw and Billie Holiday broke musical racial barriers.

However, Billie suffered constant racial indignities while travelling with an all-white band. She was refused entry into diners, hotels, and other accommodations. She could not sit at the bar and mix with customers. Artie and the band members objected to Billie Holiday's treatment, but she was treated poorly. After enduring months of racial indignities, Billie grew frustrated; she complained about sleeping accommodations; eventually she expressed her desire to quit.

Helen Forrest, a white 19-year-old singer, was hired to learn the tunes and allow the band to keep Billie longer. Helen sang with the band for gigs where clubs refused to allow Billie Holiday to sing. Helen felt Billie's ballads were not necessarily well suited for her. Billie sang most songs. Helen and Billie got along well. On top of the racial tensions, the band was not making enough money touring.

Artie recalled that during one performance, Billie went to the crook of the piano to sing, and a red neck yelled, "Let the nigger wench sing another song." Artie declared, "He didn't mean it badly. That was his designation for a Black woman." Artie tried to keep Billie quiet. Her response was loud "motherf - -er[42]." Artie Shaw often paid a couple of police officers to stand guard outside the venue in case something happened since Billie was hotheaded. Before tensions boiled over, Artie and the band hustled Billie outside, put her on the bus, and they drove off.

Artie Shaw, New York, N.Y. 1946–1948, Library of Congress

In another southern ballroom, a man yelled to Shaw, "When's blackie going to sing?" Billie Holiday yelled, "Get that motherfucker out of here.[43]" The band kept playing but Shaw singled for the band members to get ready to leave soon. Even though discrimination was relentless in the south, bigotry existed in the north too. Billie Holiday noted that she could not walk through the front door of the Lincoln Hotel in Manhattan. She could not sit at the bar and mingle with patrons there either. This luxurious hotel was built in 1928 on 44th to 45th Street and Eighth Avenue.

It was 27 stories tall and contained 1,331 rooms. The exterior contained a brick and terracotta façade.

Touring with an all-white band left Billie isolated on an island by herself. The band members enjoyed all the benefits of their whiteness. They could enter the front of fancy hotel lobbies, sit down for a meal at any counter, and even sit at the bar after a performance and issue out autographs to admiring fans. Most owners and managers of white establishments viewed Billie Holiday as a second rated Negro singer who did not deserve common courtesies.

Dressing, eating, and sleeping on the bus and being called different racial epithets and being mocked got old. Billie Holiday accused Artie Shaw of being arrogant because he tried to get her to go along to get along when it came to southern customs. She refused to sign a five-year contract to play with Shaw's orchestra and ended her tour with the band. Billie left the Artie Shaw Orchestra.

After Billie left the band, Helen Forrest recorded 38 songs including her greatest hits, *They Say* and *All The Things You Are* with the Artie Shaw Band.

In September of 1938, Holiday recorded a single, *I'm Gonna Lock My Heart*, it ranked 6th that month. Her record label, Vocalion Records, listed *I'm Gonna Lock My Heart* as its 4th bestselling record during that period. Vocalion acquired Brunswich Records in 1924; it issued a single *Cross Road Blues* by Mississippi Song Writer, Guitarist, and Blues Singer Robert Johnson. Touring across the country with the Count Basie Orchestra and the Artie Shaw Orchestra helped Billie Holiday obtain national exposure. More audiences were falling in love with her singing style. She was standing out front, shining and glowing like the moonlight.

Lester Young, Spotlite (Club), New York, N.Y. Sept. 1946
photo by William P Gottlieb, Library of Congress

Lester "Prez" Young labeled Billie Holiday "Lady Day" because he viewed her as the top jazz vocalist. White society did not accept Black women as ladies. Billie was classy. Audiences respected her. She was polite, friendly, posed, and graceful. But her mannerism among her peers was hip. She was streetwise and witty. She could out-drink men at jam sessions and house parties. Yet, she had a gentle side; she loved children, and she was sweet. She enjoyed taking children shopping and being active in their young lives. When Miles Davis lived next door, she insisted that Miles bring his son around often. He did. They were straight up cool with each other.

Buck Clayton by William P Gottlieb, Library of Congress

By 1939, Billie Holiday had cut 100s of records for Columbia, but record producers were becoming disinterested in booking her for new recording dates. Her recordings in that period featured Teddy Wilson and were labeled under Billie Holiday and her Orchestra. She also recorded with the Basie, Ellington, Goodman, and Teddy Hill bands depending on which band was in town and available for jam and recording sessions.

Billie recorded with Lester Young and Buck Clayton as often as possible. Sometimes, Lester Young hummed behind Billie's lyrics and accented her sound with his own special melody. Lester was her favorite musician. She was his favorite vocalist. His saxophone solo pieces were considered Billie Holiday's second voice in her 1930s Basie band recordings. Lester was a positive vibe in Billie's life.

Music critics mislabeled Billie Holiday as a blues artist. From 1935 to 1939, Billie Holiday only recorded two blues tones: *Billie's Blues* and *Long Gone Blues*. The other tunes from this period including *Those Foolish Things*, *I Cried for You*, *Who Loves You*, *He's Funny That Way*, *Them There Eyes*, and *Trav'lin All Alone* were Tin Pan Alley songs and Broadway songs. Tin Pan Alley was in the Flower District in Manhattan behind W. 28th Street between Fifth and Sixth Avenue.

As the adage declares, "The best is always in demand." Within three weeks of leaving the Artie Shaw band, Billie became the star attraction at the opening of Café Society, a new joint, which opened December 18, 1938, in a former basement speakeasy at 2 Sheridan Square in Greenwich Village on the west side of lower Manhattan. The owner, 36-year-old Barney Josephson had gotten out of the shoe sales business to open a spot where Black people and white people could sit shoulder to shoulder to enjoy music, great entertainment, and tasty food.

At that time, clubs did not allow Black and white people to mix in the audience. At the famous Cotton Club, located in the Midtown Theater District, Black people could entertain the audience on stage and Black people could work in the kitchen. But Black people could not sit in the audience and watch the show or mingle with the audience. Black entertainers were required to walk next door or across the street to use the restroom. Italian gangsters and New York club owners established those personnel policies, and that's how much they valued the Black entertainers who were bringing big business through the doors.

Billie Holiday, Hazel Scott, and Leonard Feather by William P Gottlieb, Library of Congress

For years, Café Society was the first and only integrated club in New York City. According to the book *Strange Fruit* by David Margolick, the door attendant broke traditional decorum at Café Society; door attendants wore rags and torn white gloves and stood to the side while customers opened the doors and let themselves inside. Black people and whites fraternized on stage and off stage. Black people were seated at the best tables while white patrons were seated in the rear of the room sometimes near the kitchen.

John Hammond introduced Josephson to 23-year-old jazz

singer Billie Holiday; to jazz greats such as Fletcher Henderson, Benny Goodman, Teddy Wilson, Charlie Christian; and to three boogie-woogie pianists: Albert Ammons, Pete Johnson, and Big Joe Turner. Josephson hired a White comedian named Jack Gilford to introduce the musicians and artists before they entered the stage integrating the club's stage entertainment. Billie Holiday was the opening act for Café Society for the next year.

Charles Gilmore recalled attending a packed house party in Harlem in 1938 and hearing Billie Holiday sing *Strange Fruit* to see what people thought of her new song. After Billie sang *Strange Fruit* and the lyrics sank in, the crowd got quiet; then, the song turned the party into a funeral. After Billie sang the last note, the pianist got up and walked away. No one clapped. Then, people let the lyrics sink in and they complimented Billie Holiday and encouraged her to sing the song for a larger audience.

Sadie, who was close to Billie, objected to Billie singing *Strange Fruit* because Sadie felt singing a protest song was putting Billie's life at risk. Billie said she was willing to risk her life if the song could bring positive awareness to the plight of Black people. In 1938, the NAACP's national headquarters at 69 Fifth Avenue in Manhattan removed its 6"x10" feet "A Man Was Lynched Today" sign which hung from the windows for years. The property owner succumbed to political pressure and demanded the removal of the sign. Although Billie Holiday was not a member of the NAACP, she unofficially grabbed the organization's anti-lynching cause by lighting a jumbo candle through the lyrics of *Strange Fruit* at Café Society.

John Hammond supported Civil Rights issues later, but when Billie Holiday sang *Strange Fruit*, he opposed Billie singing the song professionally. At that time, it was not the norm for artists to challenge racism through their art. Billie brushed John's contempt for her musical choice aside. As a Black woman, she experienced racism. She had to live with her conventions. She declared that John was square and that he wanted to control his artists. In another sense, Billie declared that she was in control of her art. She had always picked the songs and the musicians for her recordings. She decided she was taking a stance even though her mother and her record producer objected.

Sadie Fagan, Billie Holiday, mother and daughter, mid-40s

Billie Holiday's performance of *Strange Fruit* received reviews in the press. Harry Anslinger sent word for Billie Holiday to stop singing *Strange Fruit*. She responded to his request by going on stage, closing her set with *Strange Fruit,* and haunting more white listeners when she hollered 'croooooop.' She let the head of the Federal Bureau of Narcotics know she was a free agent with a lot of nerves.

Billie Holiday: Jazz Singer

Billie Holiday's refusal to concede to Harry was catastrophic. She picked a fight with one of the most powerful law enforcement officials in the nation. The legal system and public policies are an arm of the enormously powerful. Harry Anslinger was in the ranking with J. Edgar Hoover who headed the FBI. Musician Charles Mingus argued that drugs had nothing to do with the government's pursuit of Billie Holiday. As Jo Jones noted Billie Holiday's drug usage never harmed anyone. Charles Mingus felt Billie Holiday was a target of the government for singing *Strange Fruit* because the song could incite riots. Freedom of speech was not absolute. The media and power structure censored the voices of minorities. Today there are book bans.

Billie exaggerated and told people *Strange Fruit* was written especially for her; she resented any singer singing *Strange Fruit*. Ethel Waters once fell out with Billie Holiday for singing her popular tune *Stormy Weather*. However, many artists are cover singers. Ethels Waters, Billie Holiday, Lena Horne, Nat King Cole, Frank Sinatra, Etta James, Chaka Khan, and Christina Aguilera all sung the popular tune *Stormy Weather*.

Barney Josephson treated Billie Holiday's performance of *Strange Fruit* as a recital of art at a theater. Barney and Billie established reverence for her performance. Before Billie sang *Strange Fruit*, all service at Café Society came to a halt. Only a pianist and a trumpet player accompanied Billie when she sang. The waiters, cashiers, and busboys stopped working and the lights were turned off except for the spotlight pointed on Billie Holiday. When she finished, she walked off the stage and she never returned for a bow. Josephson's staff turned the lights off for effect after she finished the song. The club was quiet when Billie sang the last line, "Here is a strange and bitter *'croooooop*.'" She stretched out the word 'crop' with an extended elevated holler. *Strange Fruit* became Billie's signature song, and it was her closing song.

The waiters encouraged noisy customers to pay and leave. Barney Josephson brilliantly helped orchestrate complete reverence for the song and the floor show. Barney Josephson described Billie Holiday as "meticulous about her work." If an accompanist "played a note that disturbed her while she was singing, she picked a bone with him later. Like her surrogate brother Lester, Billie had keen ears. If the piano was one note behind or too fast, she picked it up. If she wasn't satisfied, she let them know[44]." Like his father, Willis, Lester Young used to point out the imperfections of artists too.

One night Billie Holiday was disgusted with an inattentive audience, and she got up, turned her back to the audience, lifted her dress and showed them her black ass. Josephson asked her not to be ugly to an audience again. Billie replied, "Fuck em." But she respected the establishment and fans and never showed her ass to the audience again. Show business is not perfect, but most audiences respected the song and Billie's deliverance of it. She loved her fans.

The year Billie Holiday became the featured singer at Café Society, Hitler invaded Poland which started WWII. Jewish businesses in Germany were forced to close. Domestically, the KKK terrorized Black people and held distain for Jews and gay people. There was only one Black USA congressman - Oscar Stanton De Priest from Illinois in the country. No anti-lynching legislation survived long enough to make it to the president's desk.

Barney Josephson, Founder, Café Society, 1940s

Lynchings, carried out by mob vigilantes, represented a key flaw in America's judicial system. Lynch mobs took the law into their own hands and executed victims without a judge or a jury trial. The jury system was a sham too because there were no Black jurors, especially in the south, where Black people could not vote. Since, only voter registrants could serve on juries, Black people were not privy to serve in the jury selection process or on juries as peers.

The word 'lynch' was first used in the 1800s. The practice of killing a person by lynching comes from the Lynch Law which originated through a judicial system operated by Captain William Lynch, a planter who ran a judicial tribunal in Virginia, where he tried suspects. Later, lynching was associated with the execution of individuals outside of the court system known as "trial by mob." The mob determined guilt and administered the execution. In the 1930s, every Negro in America knew or heard of an execution of an innocent man or woman by a white mob. The Black conscience opposed mob justice in any shape form or fashion.

While a few doors opened, many doors were slammed shut in the faces of Black Americans. In 1939, Pres. Roosevelt appointed William Henry Hastie as the first Black USA federal judge. Hastie later taught at Howard University School of Law. The famous NAACP lawyer Thurgood Marshall was one of his students.

In entertainment, Ethel Waters became the first Black woman to host a variety show on television on NBC. Internationally known Negro opera singer, Marian Anderson was denied the right to sing in Constitution Hall in Washington, D.C. She had to sing outside in below freezing weather. However, her fanbase gathered outside in the harsh weather to hear her sing.

Way Down South, a 1939 film, was co-written by Renaissance Poet Langston Hughes making him the first black to help write a movie script for a full 1-hour movie. This musical featured Black actors playing unintelligent

Billie Holiday: Jazz Singer

and subservient slave roles on a Louisiana plantation. The plot centered around a new slave owner planning to sell the large group of enslaved Africans. But a judge prohibited the sale. In the end, the Africans were jubilant that they could remain on the plantation with the nice master. Though Langston Hughes became a trailblazer as a script writer, the film was a very unrealistic portrayal of the happiness of the enslaved. Hughes never obtained the opportunity to co-write a screen play again.

Abel Meerepol, a Jewish English teacher at De Witt Clinton High School in the Bronx authored the poem *Strange Fruit*. He was inspired to write the poem after seeing a famous photograph of the lynching of Thomas Shipp and Abram Smith in Marion, Indiana on Thursday, August 7, 1930. Abel was haunted for days after seeing the hideous lynching photograph. Then, he penned *Bitter Fruit,* which was renamed *Strange Fruit*. The New York Teacher published *Strange Fruit* in his pseudonym name, "Lewis Allan," which represented the names of his two stillborn children. The Marxist journal, *New Masses* published *Strange Fruit*.

Abel Meerepol was a remarkably effective English teacher. He installed a love for poetry and writing in his students. Three of his students became famous. Paddy Chayefsky became an Academy award-winning screenwriter. Neil Simon became a playwright; and James Baldwin became a famous Black novelist, writer, and activist. Abel was a trade union activist; historians dubbed him a low-key member of the Communist Party.

The photograph of the lynching of Thomas Shipp and Abram Smith revealed cheerful and stone-faced White onlookers facing the photographer standing around the lifeless bodies of Thomas and Abram which were hanging from ropes stretched around the limbs of a massive tree limb on the courthouse lawn in Marion, Indiana. Thomas and Abram's clothes were torn and full of blood stains. According to the youngest and surviving teen, James Cameron, Thomas, and Abram murdered a white man, Claude Deeter, but they did not rape his alleged girlfriend Mary Ball which was the main reason the lynch mob overtook the jailer, took the teenagers from jail, and beat, tortured, mutilated, and lynched them.

Someone in the crowd helped 14-year-old James, the youngest, flee the mob. The bodies of Thomas and Abram hung on the ropes for hours attracting thousands. Photographer Lawrence Beitler stayed up 10 days and 10 nights printing and selling post cards which he made from the lynching photo of Thomas Shipp and Abram Smith. White lynching witnesses purchased post cards as souvenirs and mailed the cards to family and friends across the country.

The following Saturday, the weekly edition of the *Indianapolis Recorder* revealed that a female leader of the Marion NAACP Chapter, Katherine "Flossie" Bailey, called the sheriff, Jacob Campbell, three hours before the lynching and warned him that a mob was planning to break the teens out of jail. He went to the jail and discovered that the mob had disabled the transport vehicles. But the sheriff did not make any effort to remove the teens from the jail to prevent the mob from taking justice into their own hands. The next day, the sheriff pulled the bodies down from the ropes; mob participants cut pieces of the cloth from the deceased blood-stained clothes as souvenirs in the presence of the sheriff.

Billie Holiday: Jazz Singer

New York NAACP leader Walter White investigated the lynching and sent 27 names and evidence of their participation in the lynchings to Republican Gov. Harry G. Leslie and Attorney General James M. Ogden. Seven were arrested; two were tried by a jury. Relatives of Mary Ball admitted Thomas Shipp and Abram Smith were innocent of rape charges. Plus, Claude was not engaged to Mary. The jury acquitted both defendants of their criminal charges. Indiana whites got away with murdering – two Negroes in custody who were falsely accused of rape.

Mrs. Bailey pushed for the removal of Sheriff Campbell. But Sheriff Campbell kept his job. Mrs. Bailey successfully led an effort to get the State of Indiana to pass anti-lynching legislation in 1931. She also supported the NAACP's national anti-lynching campaign which was unsuccessful[45].

Abel Meerepol wanted his poem to become a song. After hearing Billie Holiday sing at Café Society, Abel assumed she was the perfect person to sing it. He discussed his idea with Barney Josephson. Then, they showed it to Billie; she loved it because an anti-lynching song represented a stance against American racism, and it also represented her stance against discriminatory medical policies which led to the demise of her father Clarence in 1937. Billie helped Sonny White turn the poem into lyrics for a song.

At Café Society, one could hear a pin drop when Billie Holiday finished her show. The lyrics had a profound effect on listeners. Columnists wrote about Billie Holiday's performance which attracted more people to Café Society. Café Society patrons often asked where they could purchase the *Strange Fruit* record which prompted Billie Holiday to try to get it recorded. A few white patrons complained that they had not patronized the establishment to hear *Strange Fruit* which they considered poor entertainment and walked out.

Columbia Records refused to record *Strange Fruit*. One day, Billie stopped by Commodore Music Shop which sold rare jazz records in Manhattan and asked the owner Milt Gabler if he could use his Commodore Records label to record *Strange Fruit*. Gabler and Commodore co-founder, Jack Crystal, father of the legendary actor and comedian Billy Crystal, recorded Billie Holiday singing *Strange Fruit*, *Yesterdays*, *Fine and Mellow*, and *I Gotta Right to Sing the Blues* with Billie's Café Society band. She wrote the lyrics for *Fine and Mellow*. *Strange Fruit* made it to No. 16 on the charts in July of 1939 rendering Billie Holiday, a celebrity, a race woman, and an anti-lynching activist.

Commodore Records recorded other jazz pieces including music featuring Lester Young, Buck Clayton, Freddie Green, Jo Jones, and Eddie Durham. Commodore Records reissued the piano solos of Teddy Wilson and so-so sessions of Fletcher Henderson featuring Clarence Holiday. Billie Holiday also redid *How Am I to Know? My Old Flame*, *I'll Get By*, *I Cover the Waterfront*, *Embraceable You* with Commodore. Her singing mood was cool and emotional.

Even though *Strange Fruit* was banned from air waves on many radio stations, Billie Holiday's 1939 recording of *Strange Fruit* sold over one million copies. Billie Holiday was proud of the political stance she took. She said confidently, "I am a race woman.[46]" Occasionally, Billie Holiday cried after she sang *Strange Fruit*. The horrors inflicted on Black bodies were deeply personal to her.

Billie Holiday: Jazz Singer

Researchers argued that Billie Holiday never saw a lynching in person. But she heard about lynchings. The stories of lynchings are vivid enough for any member of the Black race to feel the pain of a man who looks like one's uncle, daddy, cousin, friend, or neighbor's lifeless body hanging from a tree. Story tellers have brought lynching events to life.

Billie Holiday held stories in her bosom under her heartbeat about injustice in America. Every Black man, woman, or child living and breathing in the United States during Jim Crow heard stories about Black bodies and white terror. It was everywhere. Still is. Jazz greats as well as any Negro could turn a corner on 126th Street and meet white terror just as well as one could meet white terror on a rural winding road in a small southern town. There were race riots in Harlem in 1935 and in 1943 over the wrongful death of Black men by white police officers.

Abel Meerepol had never witnessed a lynching either. He authored the poem based on the photograph of the lynching which vividly displayed the huge crowd of White citizens posing for a photographer while the deceased bodies hung from the noose with blood drippings covering the front of their clothes.

By 1939, according to some reports the number of lynchings dropped to six and by another report to three. The year Columbia Records cut Billie Holidays first recordings, there were 26 lynchings in the United States. Twenty-four victims were Black and two were white. The 14th Amendment to the United States Constitution guarantees citizens the right to due process of the laws and equal protection of the laws. Lynchings were punishment for alleged crimes without due process of law and without a jury trial. In the south, all-white jury trials offered no justice for Black people either way – jury or lynch mob.

Police brutality, police overreach, poverty, and crime were never too far away in the 20th century. Black people cannot hold our breath too long in the 21st century. Police brutality, police overreach, poverty, and crime remain too close for comfort.

In the 20th century, corruption and discrimination ran deep from the police officer to the chief of police, to the sheriff, to the prosecutor, to the local judges, and some cases to the federal judges.

Black people, especially males, were lynched and put on public display as examples of what happens when one of them gets out of line by trying to vote, being economically well-off, or displaying manhood, or looking directly at a white woman or for being accused of touching or kissing and loving a white woman. The gross mistreatment of Black people cut deep into the hearts and minds of members of the Black race.

When Billie Holiday sang, "Southern trees bear a strange fruit. Blood on the leaves and blood at the root," she saw imagery of Black bodies swinging from ropes off the road or in the woods. She saw her father being denied medical service for his lungs. She heard the white male in the audience calling her a "Nigger wench."

Time Magazine denounced *Strange Fruit* as propaganda for the NAACP, even though Billie Holiday was not a member of the NAACP. She was a member of the jazz greats and the great jazz jam sessions. As the saying goes,

Billie Holiday: Jazz Singer

"There is no such thing as bad publicity." Columnists penned stories on the song and radio producers discussed *Strange Fruit*. A friend of Billie, John Chilton, who wrote *Billie's Blues*, said Café Society was the happiest booking of Billie's life. Her confidence improved and her art became more sophisticated.

Strange Fruit became Billie Holiday's signature song. She delivered lyrics with immense detail. *Strange Fruit* exemplified Holiday's political disdain for lynchings and discrimination. Holiday told interviewers that her father was lynched by southern racism. Bennie Goodman determined that Billie Holiday's style changed after she added *Strange Fruit* into her song catalogue. She went from an upbeat big band swing singer to a torch singer.

Café Society had a unique atmosphere. There was no cover charge. Dinner was $1.50, beer was 25¢, and a shot of Scotch was 40¢. Even though, Black people were welcome, fewer came during the Great Depression because few had extra funds for partying. Therefore, most patrons were White. The first show started at 9:30. The next set was at midnight. The last show was at 2:30 a.m. Billie's popularity soared among white intellectuals and gay people. Billie's weekly income increased to $75.00 a week[47]. After a year, the club experienced an economic downturn.

> I remember when she opened at Café Society, in December 1939, for her first big nightclub break. She was simply shocking in her impact. Standing there with a spotlight on her great, sad, beautiful face, a white gardenia in her hair, she sang her songs, and the singers were never the same thereafter[48].

89

Ralph J. Gleason, Celebrating the Duke, page 80.

In 1939, Billie Holiday and Arthur Herzog, Jr. co-wrote *God Bless the Child* which is now an iconic jazz tune. *It was* her first record to sell a million copies.

Billie Holiday's first marriage, at age 25, on Christmas Day in December of 1940, was to Trombonist Jimmy Monroe, in Elkton, Maryland. Billie was dating Pianist Sonny White when she started seeing Jimmy. Billie and Sonny broke up over her new friendship with Jimmy. Sonny did not harbor any ill feelings toward Billie. Billie's bandmates adored her.

Billie worked at Café Society until early 1940. Sister Rosetta Tharpe, the first instrumentalist to use the guitar for melody-plucked line, reached a new audience in 1940 at Café Society. Her innovative guitar skills invented the Rock and Roll guitar. She was the first commercially successful gospel singer. Chuck Berry and Elvis Presley stood on Sister Rosetta Tharpe's shoulders. Sister Rosetta Tharpe, a native of Cotton Plant, Arkansas, was born the same month and year as Billie Holiday; both were four years younger than Big Joe Turner.

Billie Holiday's associates noted that Jimmy smoked opium and was a heavy drinker and when they married, Billie Holiday advanced from smoking marijuana to smoking opium and using cocaine. Jimmy was a flashy dressing cat. Sadie did not like Jimmy. She wanted Billie to marry Sonny. But Billie Holiday chose Jimmy.

Jimmy's brother Clark Monroe owned a nightclub called Clark Monroe's Uptown House at 198 West 134th Street in Harlem. Clark was a player and a pimp, who had a good business mind. Jazz musicians such as Max Roach,

Billie Holiday: Jazz Singer

Charlie Parker, and Victor Coulsen held jam sessions at Monroe's Uptown House. Stunning bebop sounds were born during those jam sessions. Clark opened The Spotlight in 1944. In 1936, when Charlie Parker was 16, he studied Lester Young's first recorded solo *Shoeshine Boy* to improve his saxophone playing style. Charlie studied the recording note for note. By 1940, Charlie and others were creating the bebop genre. Charlie Parker became the most influential jazz icon in history.

Charlie Parker and Dizzy Gillespie ushered in the bebop jazz genre using complex, fast chords and key changes and instrumental solos. Saxophonist Lester Young's instrumental style was a forerunner to the Bebop genre. Nat King Cole and Buddy Rich were sidemen during the swing era in a trio led by Lester Young. Nat King Cole was a prominent jazz pianist and vocalist. He later launched a successful solo career. His vocals for jazz and pop songs like *Straighten Up and Fly Right*, *Sweet Lorraine*, *It's Only a Paper Moon*, and *I Love You For Sentimental Reasons* climbed the charts.

Monroe's Uptown House's house band included Max Roach, George Threadwell, and Victor Coulsen. Jimmy had multiple extra marital affairs and Billie Holiday had a toxic relationship with him. As the blues lyrics declare, *What's good for the goose is good for gander*. Billie had affairs too. In 1945, 30 year old Billie Holiday became involved with the trumpet player Joe Guy, age 25; it was widely rumored that she had an affair with Tallulah Bankhead, a successful white actress who earned $50,000 per film in the 1930s. *Variety* magazine awarded Bankhead *Best Actress of the Year* for her role in *The Little Foxes* in 1939.

Billie Holiday and her dog Boxer 1946, by William P Gottlieb, Library of Congress.

Joe and Billie became heroin addicts. Although Billie claimed in her biography *Lady Sings the Blues* that a white man in Dallas named Speck introduced her to heroin. Her friends believed she first used heroin with Joe Guy. There is debate that she introduced Joe to heroin.

A friend of Billie Holiday, James 'Stump' Cross, a comedian, recalled seeing Billie Holiday use heroin and cocaine at the same time. Then, she popped pills and washed the pills down with Scotch. James declared, "She could consume more stimulants than 10 men and still perform. She was an extremist[49]."

Joe Guy and Billie Holiday devised a scheme to avoid being busted for possession of narcotics. James 'Stump' recalled, "All the doormen along 52nd Street had what

Lady needed." Joe walked up 8th Avenue every day with Billie's dog Boxer to score an ounce of drugs. He pinned the drugs under Boxer's collar. Then, he gave a white doorman a tip to take Boxer up to Billie who was waiting in one of the hotel rooms with her wealthy friends.

Agent Jimmy Fletcher said the government was observing their scheme but was not able to get a clean arrest on Billie for years. Jimmy Fletcher was an "archive man" responsible for determining who was selling drugs, who was supplying the drugs, and recommending who the agency should bust. Eventually, Jimmy posed as a drug dealer and sold drugs to individuals in Harlem to gain their confidence.

Allegedly, Tallulah, Billie, and other actors drank and indulged in excessive drug usage. The 2021 movie *United States vs. Billie Holiday* depicted the friendship of Billie and Tallulah, who walked arm and arm in one scene through Central Park. Tallulah and Hattie McDaniel, the Black actor, whose role as Mammy in the 1939 movie *Gone With the Wind,* landed Hattie the Academy Award for Best Supporting Actress in 1940 were rumored to have belonged to the Sewing Circle, a secretive group of lesbian and bisexual Hollywood actors. Although interracial relationships of any kind were off-limits in the 1940s, Tallulah was rumored to have been romantically involved with several famous Black women. She denied it. But she was openly a lesbian. Billie was bisexual.

During the segregated ceremony, in Los Angeles, the multi-talented Hattie McDaniel had to sit at a table on the side of the room away from the other awardees and guests. Hattie McDaniel was the youngest daughter of two former enslaved Africans. She was twice widowed and twice divorced. She had an entertainment history. She was one of the first Negro women featured on the radio. She was a comedian, a gospel artist, a song writer, and one of the featured female Black actors who worked regularly in Hollywood films.

Joe Louis lands a punch against Arturo Godoy during the fight at Yankee Stadium, Bronx, New York. June 20, 1940.

On October 8, 1940, Josephson moved Café Society from Greenwich Village to East 58th St. Then, the Park Avenue crowd started walking through the doors. Eventually, the club's audience became more diverse. Famous Black Ralph Bunche, Richard Wright, Sterling Brown, Langston Hughes, Paul Robeson, and the Heavyweight boxing champion Joe Lewis, the pride of Harlem, became regular patrons. First Lady Eleanor Roosevelt even dropped in.

Sister Rosetta Tharpe and Joe Sullivan's band performed with the local boogie-woogie pianists. Young Lena Horne worked at Café Society too. Lena started working in the Cotton Club chorus at age 16 in 1933, the year Billie Holiday recorded her first record.

Billie Holiday: Jazz Singer

The lyrics in *Strange Fruit* put Abel Meerepol on the political radar. Anti-lynching advocates sent copies of *Strange Fruit* to congressmen to encourage them to write anti-lynching bills. The southern United States Democrats initiated an attack on Abel because they did not like the lyrics of *Strange Fruit*.

In 1940, Abel was called to testify before a congressional committee which was investigating communism. One of the committee members insinuated that the Communist Party paid Abel to write *Strange Fruit*. Abel was not paid to write the poem; he wrote it because he felt lynchings were grossly inhumane. Billie Holiday sang the protest song *Strange Fruit* from 1939-1959. *Strange Fruit* was a forerunner protest song to the protest songs produced afterward such as *A Change Gotta' Come* by Sam Cooke and *Mississippi Goddam* by Nina Simone.

From 1940 to 1942, Billie Holiday was the headliner for the Lionel Hampton band. Lionel Leo Hampton, a jazz vibraphonist, pianist, and percussionist split with the Benny Goodman Orchestra and formed his own band in 1940. Lionel was a big name in the swing genre. Billie also made special appearances with Count Basie's band. In 1941, Billie Holiday performed on the same bill at the Palace Theater in Cleveland, Ohio with teenager singer Dinah Washington, who admired Billie.

Music promoter Joe Glazer developed a relationship with local law enforcement agents who asked him to tell Billie the U.S.A. government wanted her to cease singing the protest song *Strange Fruit*. Billie Holiday popularized *Strange Fruit* a mere two years after the U.S.A. congress refused to pass a bill written to make lynchings a federal crime. Southern congressmen used the filibuster to block the passage of the bill.

Harry Anslinger, FBN Commissioner, Library of Congress

Harry Anslinger, the first commissioner of the Federal Bureau of Narcotics (FBN), hired a Black agent, Jimmy

Billie Holiday: Jazz Singer

Fletcher, to keep an eye on Billie Holiday. Harry Anslinger was a former prohibition agent whose assignment was hunting down and locking up alcohol dealers. Harry headed the Federal Bureau of Prohibition until 1933. The agency failed to reduce the massive bootlegging business during Prohibition. Fletcher established a fake fan friendship with Billie and warned Billie to stop singing *Strange Fruit* too. The repeated warnings to Billie to stop singing the lynching protest song went in one of her ears and out the other one.

Jazz was popular and the music was integrating the races. The White Power structure did not want the races to mix. The year before Billie Holiday's birth, *The New York Times* ran an article, Sunday, February 8, 1914, entitled *Negro Cocaine 'Fiends' New Southern Menace*, to cause the public to fear Black drug users. The article insinuated that southern Negroes were sniffing cocaine. "The drug [dry cocaine] produces an exhilaration which is usually simply a mind intoxication, although it may produce the wildest form of insane excitation, accompanied by the fantastic hallucinations and delusions that characterize acute mania.[50]" The report which proposed Negroes turned to dried cocaine during prohibition because they could not get whiskey was a big fat fake rumor. However, the news created hysteria. That year, the federal government banned the use of Heroin and Cocaine.

Finding southern Negroes snorting cocaine in 1914, was like finding a needle in haystack. Any farmhand or sharecropper of any color knew how to ferment fruit from any tree to make home make wine or brew. Nathan "Nearest" Green, an enslaved African, born around 1820, was the best skilled whiskey distiller in the 1850s in Lynchburg, Tennessee. Jack Daniel took credit for inventing the whiskey Nearest created and named it after himself. During and after slavery, free and enslaved African males were skilled in all industries. African labor built this country. Africans arrived here skilled.

Law enforcement was concerned about race mixing because white males did not want Negroes, Mexicans, or Chinese immigrants to have access to white women. Harry Anslinger alleged he feared all non-white males planned to use drugs to lure white girls and then take advantage of them.

Based on the findings of *Chasing the Scream*, on July 6, 1927, the *New York Times* ran a story targeting Mexicans too. The headlines read *Mexican Family Go Insane*. The story declared that a widow and her four children were driven insane after eating a Marihuana plant which they pulled from their garden. Harry Anslinger was pro-marijuana until he received word that Negro students were partying with white girls.

Whites feared that the next act was interracial relationships and biracial children. Harry Anslinger asked a group of scientists to give their findings on the dangers of marijuana use. He quoted the negative findings of one scientist and ignored the other scientists to prove his point. It was well known that Negro jazz musicians had love affairs with white women. Lester Young, Quincy Jones, Miles Davis, Harry Belafonte, Sammy Davis Jr., and Charles Mingus had interracial relationships with white women. Several men fathered children with their white wives, and they were present fathers. White males fathered children with Black women for 350 years and were not present in the households of their Black families leaving millions of offspring disinherited.

Sensational propaganda claimed marijuana was "Weed with Roots in HELL" that led to ORGIES WILD PARTIES and UNLEASHES PASSIONS[51]. The Marijuana Tax Act was enacted in 1937 which made it hard to legally possess and sell all forms of cannabis in the United States. The Marijuana Tax Act was disproportionately enforced against people of color.

Harry Anslinger claimed Mexican immigrants and Black people were using drugs more than whites across the nation. Then, he claimed drug use increased interracial dating and race mixing. Allegedly, the mafia paid Harry to keep his agents away from them enabling them to maintain control of one of the largest underworld and profitable markets in the United States. The underworld leaders encouraged Harry to launch the War on Drugs. Politicians in Washington did not want agents to target white entertainers or musicians. The mission of FBN was a daunting task of ending the drug trade.

The War on Drugs was the scam of the 20th century. When Billie arrived in Harlem in 1928 at age 13, it was legal to buy, sell, and smoke marijuana. At the time of her birth anyone could buy drugs worldwide. Americans could buy products over the counter at their local pharmacy containing morphine and cocaine such as paregoric which was used for babies. Every ounce of Mrs. Winslow's Soothing Syrup, a popular cold medicine, contained .65 millimeters of morphine. Opiates, morphine, and heroin were sold at pharmacies. Before prohibition, 22 percent of drug addicts were wealthy. In comparison, only 6 percent of addicts were poor[52]. Pharmacies charged two or three cents for a grain of morphine. Once criminal gangs controlled the drug market, they marked the price up from a few pennies to $1.00.

Harry Anslinger allegedly helped smuggle drugs into the country which were sold to addicts. By the mid-1920s, Jewish Crime Boss Arnold Rothstein and the New York gangs controlled the entire heroin and cocaine market along the Eastern seaboard. After the drug trade transferred to the underworld, Arnold could be spotted standing in Times Square with his thugs near the jazz clubs looking for people who owed him money. The drug trade was lucrative. The World newspaper reported, "For every $1,000 spent in purchasing opium, smuggling it into the country and dispersing it, those at the top of the pyramid collect $6,000 or more in profit.[53]"

The top dealers could easily afford to pay off police officers. And they did. During prohibition, New York's police's pockets were lined with money from Speakeasy owners. The underworld corrupted law enforcement by providing them with regular payoffs. Arnold was so powerful that his murder charges vanished. In Southern centers, power and corruption were centered on the agenda of the Klu Klux Klan. In Northern centers, power and corruption aligned with the agenda of the underworld.

Under Harry Anslinger's leadership, the War on Drugs became a war against the Black and brown community especially jazz musicians. Perhaps, Harry posted Billie Holiday's face on the wall at his office and threw a dart square on her face. The FBN spent years of resources and manpower on the destruction of Billie Holiday after she refused to stop singing *Strange Fruit*. Jimmy Fletcher infiltrated Billie's inner circle; thereby defining the playbook used years later, to name a few, on Malcolm X, Martin Luther King Jr., leaders of the Black Panther Party,

Billie Holiday: Jazz Singer

and anyone challenging the American social, economic, and political power structure.

According to *Chasing the Scream: The First and Last Days of the War on Drugs*, Harry Anslinger hated jazz music. He wrote in his notes of jazz, "It sounded like the jungles in the dead of night." He added, "It reek of filth." His agents reported that jazz musicians played under the influence of marijuana. Anslinger analyzed music lyrics as evidence that intoxicated Black people would have a negative influence on society. He and his agents dissected the lyrics from the song, *That Funny Refer Man*[54]. Cab Calloway sang *The Funny Refer Man*. One lyric said, "Any time he takes a notion, he can walk across the ocean." In other words, Black and brown intoxicated weed users believed they could walk the water.

Harry advised his agents before they made a raid "Shoot first." Harry Anslinger's war on drugs originally targeted jazz musicians. But the musicians refused to snitch on each other, and they raised money to bail each other out of jail when they were arrested. Anslinger wrote to his agents, "Please prepare all cases in your jurisdiction involving musicians in violation of the marijuana laws. We will have a great national round-up arrest of all such persons on a single day[55]." He planned to do a large publicity stunt, but it never materialized. When Billie Holiday started singing *Strange Fruit*, Anslinger started focusing on Lady Day and dropped the agency's collective focus on the jazz community at large.

Famed Black Author James Baldwin wrote, "It is only in his music, which Americans are able to admire because protective sentimentality limits their understanding of it, that the Negro in America has been able to tell his story.[56]"

Billie Holiday's deliverance of *Strange Fruit* was a game changer. She revised the social contract between Black singers and white audiences by shedding light on social justice stories through song which was taboo politically and socially even in conversation. The lyrics of *Strange Fruit* prompted emotions in listeners.

Strange Fruit Lyrics

Southern trees bear a strange fruit
Blood on the leaves and blood at the root
Black bodies swinging in the Southern breeze
Strange fruit hanging from the poplar trees

Pastoral scene of the gallant south
The bulging eyes and the twisted mouth
Scent of magnolias, sweet and fresh
Then the sudden smell of burning flesh

Here is a fruit for the crows to pluck
For the rain to gather, for the wind to suck
For the sun to rot, for the tree to drop
Here is a strange and bitter crop[57]

Holiday's first recording of *Strange Fruit* sold 20,000 copies. The song has been reissued multiple times and record sales remain high. Lena Horne and Ethel Kitt felt *Strange Fruit was* too painful to sing. Paul Robeson hated the song. On August 7, 1941, Okeh Records, a subsidiary of Columbia Records recorded *Gloomy Sunday* and *God Bless the Child*, two of Holiday's storytelling songs. Paul Robertson sang *Gloomy Sunday* in the United Kingdom before Billie recorded it. But *Gloomy Sunday* became her legendary tune worldwide. *Gloomy Sunday* which discussed a lover preparing to commit suicide, *Strange Fruit*, *I Cover the Waterfront*, and *Love for Sale* were Billie

Billie Holiday: Jazz Singer

Holiday tunes banned by U.S.A. radio stations.

Gloomy Sunday verse song by Billie Holiday:

> Gloomy is Sunday, with shadows I spend it all
> My heart and I have decided to end it all[58]

Regardless of Billie's personal failings and her troubles with authorities she continued to make great music. She headlined at the Apollo with Duke Ellington, Count Basie, Fletcher Henderson, and Louis Armstrong. During this period, Billie sang Tin Pan Alley songs such as *I Cried for You*, *I Cover the Waterfront*, *I Wished on the Moon*, *My Man*, and *Lover, Come Back to Me*. Holiday restructured the lyrics in *I Cried for You* and *Summertime*. In 1942, the Jazz Record Book dubbed *Strange Fruit* one of the six most notable recordings of Billie Holiday.

Billie Holiday was a heroine for social justice in her own right. She influenced the integration of jazz clubs in Los Angeles, California in 1942. She discussed over her tears with Norman Granz, a UCLA student and Marie Bryant how disappointed she was that her Black friends could not see her perform when she was in Los Angeles. Marie Bryant was a Black singer and dancer who had collaborated with Louis Armstrong, Lionel Hampton, and Duke Ellington. Norman suggested that Billy Berg, who ran the Trouville Club, a small smoky joint, integrate his jazz club as Sunday jam sessions. Norman set the event up which went well. The Sunday jam session went so well that Billy Berg desegregated all his clubs.

The Sunday jam sessions went well but racial strife increased in the following years with the Sleepy Lagoon gang murder case and the Zoot Suit Riots which involved

Mexican Americans, African American, jazz musicians, and hipsters. Billie Holiday and jazz musicians faced discrimination often. She wanted justice for her people. She did not take it lightly that her Black friends could not sit in the audience to see her perform because they were the darker brothers and sisters. Billie Holiday became a trailblazer as the first Negro female singer in Artie Shaw's Band; she continued to influence social change.

Norman Granz, May 1947. by William P Gottlieb, Library of Congress

Billie Holiday: Jazz Singer

Four

The Decca Years

Historians dub 1939 to 1949 as the Second Billie Holiday Period. On June 12, 1942, in Los Angeles, California, Billie Holiday recorded *Trav'lin Light* for Capitol Records which was founded by Johnny Mercer, a Tin Pan Alley songwriter and record producer; Buddy DeSylva, a song writer and former film producer at Paramount; and Glenn Wallichs, owner, and Wallichs Music City record store, Hollywood, California.

On April 8, 1942, the day after Billie's 27th birthday, Capitol Records Producer Paul Whiteman used Billie Holiday's pseudonym "Lady Day" to record *Trav'lin Light* since Billie was technically under contract with Columbia Records. *Trav'lin Light* hit #23 on the pop charts and it hit #1 on the R&B charts.

Billie and her husband Jimmy Monroe travelled to Los Angeles that year and he was arrested for smuggling drugs into the State of California. During his trial Billie started working at the Trouville Club. Jimmy was found guilty of drug smuggling, and he was sentenced to serve one year in prison.

On June 25, 1944, Billie Holiday appeared on WMCA Radio Broadcast Special entitled *New World A-Coming: Inside*

105

Black America based on the best-selling book *New World A-Coming: Inside Black America* by Roi Ottley. WMCA Production collaborated with The City-Wide Citizens Committee on Harlem to create the show which starred: Billie Holiday, Art Tatum, Ben Webster, Slam Stewart, Charlie Stavers, Roy Eldridge, Edmond Hall, Benny Morton, Arthur Trappier, Vic Dickerson, Josh White, and Hall Johnson and His Choir. Canada Lee narrated the Negro musical production.

The narrator acknowledged the influence of Negro music on the United States. "Music is the Negro's greatest gift to America…The haunting overtone of the blues. The color, lift, and distinctive sophistication of jazz have all enriched the nation.[59]" The author noted that Negro music in America started in the south on the plantations during slavery. The production sampled the music of selected artists. Josh White performed first. He played his guitar and sang *I Got a Head Like a Rock and a Heart Like a Marble Stone*. Billie Holiday sang *Fine and Mellow and All of Me*. Art Tatum accompanied her.

By the summer of 1944, on August 7, 1944, Milt Gabler, Jewish record producer, signed 29-year-old Billie Holiday to Decca Records. Milt was a song writer and music pioneer; he was the first person in the industry to reissue records, the first to sell records via mail order, and the first to credit all the musicians involved in the recordings. American Actor and Comedian Billy Crystal is his nephew. *Lover Man* was her first Decca recording. It hit # 16 on the pop chart and it hit # 5 of the R&B charts. *Lover Man* was one of her biggest hits. She became popular in the pop community. Then, she was offered solo concerts which was rare for jazz singers in the 1940s. During the Decca years, Billie Holiday entered her second period as a singer. She sang lyrics slower like the pace of funeral songs.

In 1944, Commodore Records recorded Billie Holiday's version of *I'll Be Seeing You*. Songwriters Sammy Fain and Irving Kahal during WWII wrote the song when many were missing soldiers serving abroad in the war. *I'll Be Seeing You*, a sentimental ballad, was published in 1938 and it debuted in the Broadway play *Right This Way*. As John Szwed proclaimed, Billie Holiday pulls the hearts and ears of listeners when she sings the lyrics, *I'll Be Seeing You* slower than normal. This space of time gives listeners time to imagine seeing someone he or she misses sitting or standing in a familiar place; this space and time reaches the soul of the heart.

> *I'll Be Seeing You* lyrics:
>
> I'll be seeing you
> In all the old familiar places
> That this heart of mine embraces
> All day through
>
> In that small cafe
> The park across the way
> The children's carousel
> The chestnut trees
> The wishin' well[60]

In 1945, she recorded *Don't Explain, Big Stuff, What Is This Thing Called Love?* and *You Better Go Now*. The band used strings and a violin for *Don't Explain*. She was thrilled. Billie wrote *Don't Explain* after she saw lipstick on Jimmy Monroe's collar, and he tried to explain how it got on his collar. She told him to be quiet and go take a bath.

Women in Billie's audiences said they were encouraged to leave their unfaithful men after hearing Billie sing *Don't Explain*. She also recorded *Lover Man* in 1945; it hit # 5 on the R&B chart. Eventually, Jimmy and Billie were married only on paper.

Tenor Saxophonist Sonny Rollins was born in New York on September 7, 1930, when Harlem was a jazz mecca; he was influenced by jazz early in life; he was smitten with Billie Holiday and he and his friends sat and listened to her sing whenever the opportunity presented itself. "I loved her. Everybody loved Billie Holiday. She was an attractive woman. She resembled my mother," he declared[61]. He admired the Gardenia that Billie wore in her hair too. "My mother wore a flower in her hair when she took pictures. I loved my mother[62]," he added.

Sonny's parents Walter and Vallie moved their family to Sugar Hill, an upper working-class community in Harlem, when Sonny was nine. He learned to play the saxophone while he was a high school student at Benjamin Franklin High School, the first integrated high school in New York City. He loved listening to Saxophonists Coleman Hawkins, Louis Jordan, and Lester Young. "I used to go to the Apollo from school[63]," Sonny Rollins said. On those evenings, Sonny saw live performances by Duke Ellington, Ella Fitzgerald, Lionel Hampton, Dinah Washington, Fats Waller, and others.

Sonny was inspired by the great talents of his time to become a musician and bandleader. He determined, "This is the life for me[64]." Sonny's oldest sister, Gloria, played piano at a local church. His older brother Val graduated from Meharry Medical College, an HBCU in Nashville, Tennessee and became a physician, a remarkable

Billie Holiday: Jazz Singer

achievement for an immigrant from St. Thomas, W. Indies. Sonny Rollins was the youngest and only member of his family who was born in New York.

"Affluent Blacks lived in Sugar Hill in the 1930s and 1940s like the famous NAACP man WEB DuBois," Sonny Rollins said. Youth in Sugar Hill had the opportunity to see successful Black people from all social classes including authors, poets, business owners, and politicians. In Pigtown most people popping dollars were hustlers, madams, and pimps. It is true. Youth admire the successful people they see in their environment.

By the time Sonny Rollins was 19 years old, he became a recording artist. Sonny determined that "Jazz is a force of nature. It's a feeling. It's a sense of liberation[65]."

During the mid-1940s, at the height of Billie Holiday's popularity, she became openly bi-sexual. She loved Joe Guy. Their addiction was problematic. Billie Holiday noted of the cost of her addiction, "I was one of the highest paid slaves around[66]," in her biography *Lady Sings the Blues*.

Billie Holiday and Joe Guy tried to overcome their addiction. Heroin addiction is brutal like a pimp. Sadie worried about Billie's addiction. Joe was an accomplished musician. They established Billie Holiday and her Band. He was the band leader. They purchased a white bus and imprinted Billie Holiday and her Band on the side of her bus. Sadie was proud. She made curtains for the bus. She even cooked for the band before they went on overnight trips. She loved cooking. People loved her cooking. Sadie loved everyone who loved Billie. Billie was her girl.

The band took a trip to Washington, DC. After the band

finished a gig at Howard Theater, Billie had a premonition that Sadie died. She turned to Joe Guy, and told him, "Mama just left. She's dead. 'and goddamit' you better be good to me because you're all I've got.[67]" Joe Guy thought Billie was ridiculous. They had recently eaten at Sadie's apartment, and he could see her waving goodbye to the band as the bus drove off. However, Joe and Billie soon received word that Joe Glaser asked everyone not to tell Billie that Sadie died because he was going to make the funeral arrangements and notify band members when it was okay to tell Billie.

Joe Glaser made the arrangements for Sadie's funeral. When Billie arrived in New York, Joe took Billie to the funeral home. Billie was pleased with the arrangements, but she requested the funeral staff dress her mother in one of her good suits. Billie went back to Washington, DC and finished her gig. Then, she returned to New York to funeralize Sadie. Sadie was buried at Saint Raymond's Cemetery in Bronx County, NY. Billie lost her father Clarence when she was 20 years old. At the time of his death, he was 37 years old. Ten years later, at age 30, Billie lost Sadie who was age 49. Billie grieved the loss of her mother. There is nothing like a mother.

Apart from singing, Billie did not find enough positive ways to channel her energy. Joe Guy was loss himself. Hard drug usage distorted their sense of realism. Between he and Billie *the blind was leading the blind*.

Billie Holiday recorded *Good Morning Heartache* in 1946. Though it is a beautiful song, it didn't hit the charts. However, Billie won *Esquire* magazine's Gold Award for best female vocalist. She and Teddy Wilson won a poll and a trophy in 1947. There is a photograph of Billie and

Billie Holiday: Jazz Singer

Teddy standing next to Arthur Godfrey holding their trophies. Billie elevated her artistry. When she sang at the Famous Doors on 52nd Street in New York in 1942, she earned $100 per week. By the mid-1940s she was earning $1,000 per week. She recalled "I opened Café Society as an unknown and left there later as a star.[68]"

John Hammond connected Billie to her second film project which was monumental for her to sing with her musical idol Louis Armstrong. She played the role of a housekeeper alongside Louis Armstrong and Woody Herman in *New Orleans* on April 18, 1947, which was distributed by United Artist. She recorded *The Blues Are Brewin* for the soundtrack. She sang the tune beautifully. During the 90-minute film she sang, *Do You Know What It Means to Miss New Orleans?* and *Farewell to Storyville*. *New Orleans* was written by Herbert J. Biderman, a Jewish screenwriter.

Farewell to Storyville lyrics

All, you old-time queens, from new orleans,
who lived in storyville
You sang the blues, try to amuse,
here's how they pay the bill
The law step-in and call it sin to have a little fun
The police car has made a stop and storyville is done
Pick out your steamboat, pick yourself a train
- A slo-ow train[69]

Biderman was investigated for his alleged connection to the Communist party. He refused to cooperate with Congress; he was arrested for contempt of Congress. He was banned from Hollywood for a few years. But he made a comeback in 1954 when he directed the film *Salt of the*

Earth which centered around a strike led by the Hispanic wives of miners who brought attention to the deplorable working conditions of their husbands.

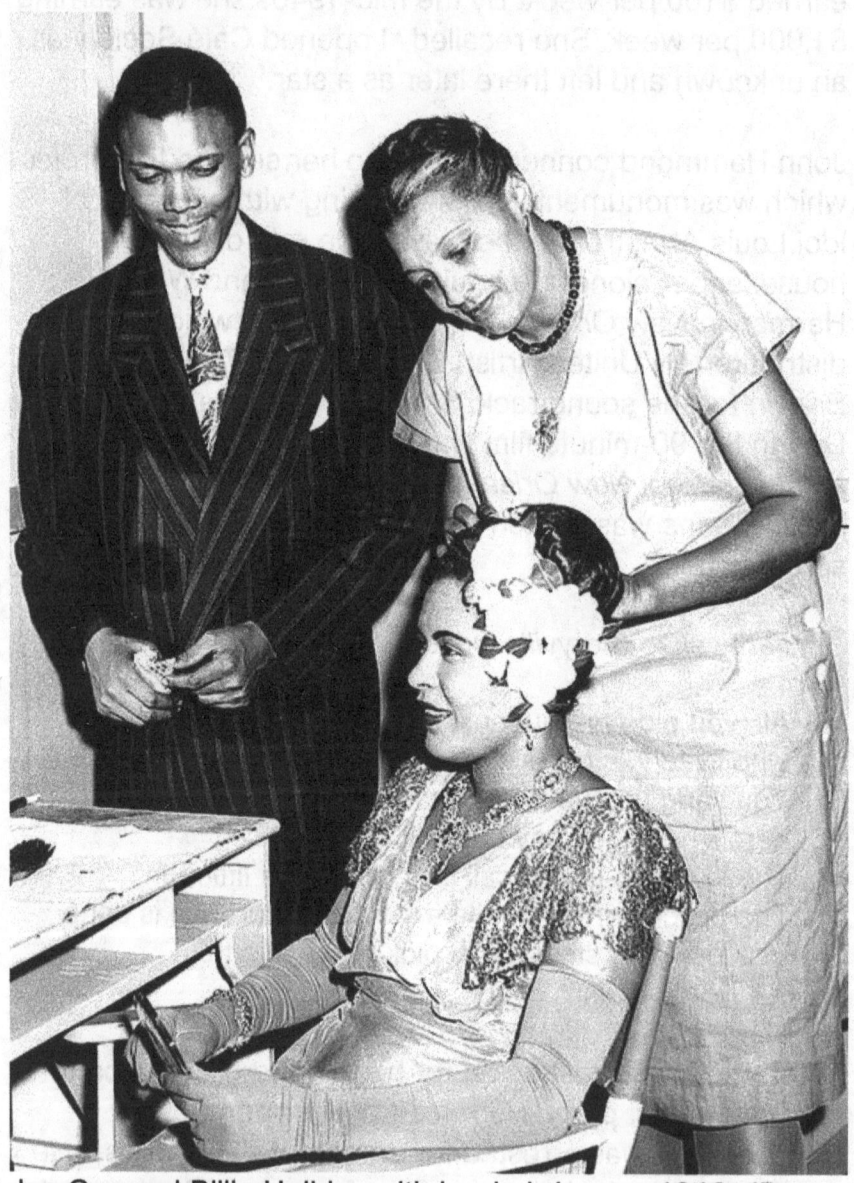

Joe Guy and Billie Holiday with her hairdresser 1946. JP Redfern's Jazz Archive.

Billie Holiday: Jazz Singer

Billie Holiday, DownBeat, 1947 by William P Gottlieb, Library of Congress.

During this time, though Billie earned $1,000 per week for her club performances, she blew it all. Her manager Joe Guy managed her money and supplied her drugs. The movie executives were aware of Billie's drug problem; so, they banned Joe from the *New Orleans* movie set. Billie reached her commercial peak in the mid-1940s; from 1944 to 1947 she earned $250,000 annually. Joe Guy who was a drug user too, spent $1,000 of her earnings each week on heroin. By then, Billie's drug usage negatively affected her work. She was late to gigs and started getting high during intermissions. She had so many needle marks on her arms that she had to cover her arms with decorative cloth and arm length gloves before her stage performances.

According to Narcotics Agent Jimmy Fletcher Joe Glaser called Anslinger's office and wanted agents to arrest Billie Holiday for her own good. He allegedly had unsuccessfully tried to help her get detoxicated. Joe felt that jail was the only way to get Billie clean. He assumed if he could save Billie, he could save his investment in her art.

In 1946, Billie Holiday won the Metronome magazine popularity poll. From 1939 to 1961, Metronome readers selected the magazine's top jazz artists and musicians through annual polls. From 1946 to 1947, Billie ranked second in the Downbeat poll; on July 6, 1947, she ranked 5th for girl singers in the Billboard Annual College poll.

The spring of 1947, Billie Holiday checked into a sanatorium in Manhattan at a tune of $2,000 to get detoxicated. Injecting heroin in one's veins is highly addictive. Her friends had tried off and on to help Billie detox by locking her in rooms hoping she could wean herself off drugs. The sanatorium treatment was supposed to be confidential. Unbeknownst to Billie Holiday, Joe Glaser was communicating with law enforcement. The day Billie was released, Joe Glaser and his secretary picked her up and his car was trailed by law enforcement. She tried to get her life together, but trouble was around the corner.

Joe Glaser was a profiteer. He launched his booking business with Louis Armstrong in 1935 when Louis Armstrong was looking for protection after being threatened by notorious New York mobster Dutch Schultz who wanted to squeeze Louis Armstrong's earnings. Joe

Billie Holiday: Jazz Singer

Glaser had dodged a statutory rape sentence in 1928 when he was running nightclubs and whorehouses on the South Side of Chicago for the underworld controlled by Al Capone. The charges forced Joe out of the nightclub business. Joe started rigging prizefights after he had to get out of the nightclub business. A booking company was the perfect new opportunity for Joe Glaser.

Joe Glaser often told people up front, "You don't know me. But you know two things about me: I have a terrible temper, and I always keep my word[70]."

From the start, Joe Glaser and Louis Armstrong's partnership was very lucrative. Joe gave up the prizefighters and made Louis's career his top priority. Joe even hired and fired band members. Joe shifted Louis's performances into mainstream American audiences through television shows, national magazines appearances, and Hollywood movies. Joe Glaser promised Louis Armstrong fame and fortune, and Joe made good on his promise. Louis Armstrong's bestselling single *Hello Dolly* hit # 1 on *Billboard Hot 100 list* in 1964. *Louis Armstrong won Best Vocal Performance, Male* in 1965. *Louis sang Hello Dolly* in the 1969 *Hello Dolly* film starring Barbara Streisand.

Joe Glaser formed the Associated Booking Corporation (ABC) following his success with Louis Armstrong. He lived well from their booking agency. He rode around in a blue convertible Rolls Royce and was a man with a luxurious lifestyle. He managed other jazz greats including Billie Holiday, Duke Ellington, others, and Joe helped them become mainstream artists too. Yes, Joe helped Joe too.

On May 6, 1947, Billie Holiday was arrested in

115

Philadelphia, in her hotel room, for possession of narcotics. FBN Agent Jimmy Fletcher set her up. He had been around her enough to gain her trust. The two had conversed. He had witnessed her drinking whiskey like a fish. Sometimes she drank gin and sometimes she drank Courvoisier. Jimmy Fletcher told Billie's biographer, Julia Blackburn, that when he raided Billie's room, he knocked on the door pretending he was delivering a telegram.

He recalled that Billie said, "Stick it under the door."

Jimmy Fletcher replied, "It's too big to go under the door."

Billie let Jimmy Fletcher in her hotel room. She was alone. Then, she discovered that Jimmy was not her fan. He was working for the man. Even though she had grown to like him and had even talked openly around him. He was a drug agent, who was sent to build a drug case against her. In Club Ebony, 1678 Broadway, New York City, Jimmy and Billie talked for hours and danced swaying to the sounds of jazz music. Jimmy suggested Billie cooperate and give him the drugs she had in her room. Billie did not concede. Billie volunteered to strip because she did not want agents to call a female to search her body. Billie striped and faced the male agents naked as a J-bird; then she urinated on the floor in front of them. Fletcher's partner sent for a female agent to conduct a body search anyway.

After the raid, Jimmy Fletcher took Billie Holiday to the side and promised to ask Anslinger to go easy on her. But Anslinger did not have any sympathy for Billie Holiday or any Black jazz artist. When Harry Anslinger was alerted that Actor Judy Garland was using heroin, he invited her to his office. He was not interested in ruining the reputation of famous white drug users. He used his resources to help

Caucasian female drug users wean themselves off hard drugs. But on the other hand, obviously Anslinger felt it was proper to lock up Black entertainers.

The result of her drug arrest was *The United States v. Billie Holiday*. On Tuesday, May 27, 1947, Billie was taken to the U.S. District Courthouse on Ninth and Market Street in Philadelphia two blocks from the Earl Theater where Billie had performed many times. During the court proceedings, she was sick and experiencing withdrawal symptoms. She could barely walk. Court officials authorized a nurse to administer a shot of morphine to help Billie sit through the proceedings. She agreed to waive the presentation of the indictment. Joe Glaser advised her to get a lawyer. She refused and represented herself even though she was sick. She pleaded guilty; then, she asked to be sent to a hospital for treatment.

The District Attorney informed the judge that Billie Holiday earned $56,000 or $57,000 the previous year and she did not have any of her earnings. The DA proposed that guys traveling with Billie scored drugs and overcharged her. They paid five or $10 for drugs and charged her $100 to $200 for the drugs. Billie Holiday was a famous singer, and she could not go to drug houses and score drugs for herself. Therefore, it was easy to take advantage of Billie Holiday. The DA proposed that Billie needed treatment so she could be cured of drugs. However, the judge rejected providing treatment for Billie and ordered her to serve one year and one day in prison. Billie was sentenced to serve time at the Federal Women's Reformatory in Alderson, West Virginia.

Billie took the drug rap for Joe Guy claiming the drugs belonged to her and that he was clean. Subsequently, he was released from jail, and he returned to his hometown of Birmingham, Alabama. Eventually, Joe played locally with Frank "Doc" Adams, a jazz clarinetist and saxophonist, who was an Alabama Jazz Hall of Fame inductee and the son of Oscar Adams, who had been a trombonist for W.C. Handy. Joe Guy publicly discussed his drug addiction and warned others about the dangers of drugs. Oscar Adams's son Oscar Adams Jr. served on the Alabama Supreme Court 1980-1993. Oscar Adams Elementary School in Gadsden, Alabama was named for him in 1983.

Billie served her time in the segregated jail. The work line included one line for Negro women and one line for White women. During Chapel and at movies white inmates sat up front and Negroes sat in the back. One thing is for sure. Billie's fans were loyal. They mailed Billie over 300 Christmas cards during the Christmas season of 1947.

Upon her release from prison, in 1948, Billie lost her cabaret license in New York City which revoked her ability to sing in nightclubs where alcohol was sold. Losing her cabaret license was a major setback. The license was revoked in part because authorities claimed listening to Billie Holiday harmed the public morals. She was devastated and felt hopeless. Her ability to sing was her bread and butter. One night Billie got drunk and cried to her friend Greer Johnson that she would never sing again. Her friend encouraged Billie to make a way to go over the bridge, or to go under the bridge. He encouraged her to make it work. She found another wind of strength.

The cabaret license was a form of discrimination used often by the police to keep jazz musicians from performing in jazz clubs and earning a living. Besides, Billie Holiday, Charlie Parker, Red Rodney, Thelonious Monk, Chev

Billie Holiday: Jazz Singer

Baker, Jackie McLean, Miles Davis, J.J. Johnson, and Dizzy Gillespie lost their cabaret license. Some artists regained their license. Billie never did. Frank Sinatra refused to go to a New York police station and get fingerprinted and photographed to apply for a cabaret license. He was able to sing in any night club without a license. He was a privileged Italian American musician. But Billie Holiday maintained her notoriety in the jazz world. She persevered, but it was not easy.

Frank Sinatra used his privilege to advance race relations in New York. After Benjamin Franklin High School on Pleasant Street in Manhattan integrated for the 1945-1946 school year, there was intense fighting between Black and Italian students. "We were bussed from Harlem to Manhattan," Sonny Rollins recalled. Italian students rejected sharing their school space with Black students. The Italians threw objects out of the window at Black newcomers and initiated physical altercations.

Sonny added, "Frank Sinatra told the Italian students to stop fighting with Black students[71]." According to Sonny Rollins, Nat King Cole sang and encouraged peace with students too. The Italian students loved Frank Sinatra and Nat King Cole. At that time, Frank Sinatra was the most famous Italian in the U.S.A. Nat King Cole's music had crossed into mainstream America.

John Levy, a Jewish gangster, who owned Club Ebony in New York City, offered Billie a gig at his club as a featured artist. However, John was a paid informer for the New York police. Billie fell into the arms of her enemy who was posing as someone who could help her get her life together and get her Cabaret license restored. On top of that, John was married with a son. But his marital status

119

did not stop Billie Holiday from falsifying her status and proclaiming to be his wife to club patrons. Linda Lipnack Huehl concluded of Billie, "She did what she wanted to do with a vengeance."

Frank Sinatra, Liederkrantz Hall, New York, N.Y., 1947.
Library of Congress

Maria Bryant, a dancer, who was a friend of Billie Holiday said John was very abusive to Billie. But she was not a doormat. Maria said John and Billie injured each other one night in a hotel room and they both had to go to the hospital. She hit him over his head with a broken coca cola bottle. Maria despised John; she called him, "a dirty, rotten, stickin' bastard[72]."

Billie Holiday, Carnegie-Hall, 1948, William P Gottlieb, Library of Congress

Don Frierman produced a Carnegie Hall event for Billie Holiday, Wednesday, November 10, 1948, after her release from prison; there were two shows (8:30 p.m. and Midnight); she received three curtain calls in front of a sold-out audience. The promotion tag was: *The Songs and Story of Miss Billie Holiday* with Coleman Hawkins, Buck Clayton, Roy Eldridge, and Al Cohn. The Chico Hamilton Quintet performed.

During rehearsal, Billie looked frail and sickly. Her legs and ankles were swollen; she looked thin in her gown. Frierman was worried Billie might not make it through the night. When the curtains were drawn, Billie stepped into the spotlight wearing a white evening gown and a white gardenia in her hair; the evening belonged to Lady Day. She sang beautifully.

Music critics predicted Sarah Vaughan, who was nine years younger than Billie Holiday was going to replace Billie as a leading voice in jazz. Sarah's career took off after she released the hit single *It's Magic on* December 27, 1947. Sarah won Esquire's New Artist Award in 1947. She won awards from *Down Beat* from 1947-1949.

But Billie Holiday reinvented herself during each of her three periods. First, she sang the big band sound in 30s and she could swing a song. Swing refers to a strong groove or drive. Swing music was danceable music. Billie Holiday sang on vocals with the kings of swing including Louis Armstrong, Coleman Hawkins, Count Basie, Jimmy Dorsey, Artie Shaw, Benny Goodman, Lester Young, Lionel Hampton, and Duke Ellington. Next, she sang ballads and torch songs.

In 1951, Cab Calloway published a piece, *Is Dope Killing*

Billie Holiday: Jazz Singer

Our Musicians? The article argued that the abundance of drugs in the Black community reduced an unmeasurable sum of jazz musicians drug addicts. New York City was the heroin Capital of the U.S.A. Whites have always been the primary users. Black addicts were criminalized, rather than rehabilitated; their cabaret cards were revoked leaving them without a means to earn a living in their trade.

Sarah Vaughan, Cafe Society, 1947, William P Gottlieb, Library of Congress

Charlie Parker pleaded with New York officials to restore

his Cabaret license. His loss of earnings further complicated his fragile life. He suffered with mental illness and substance abuse and died in New York at age 34. Dizzy Gillespie paid for Charlie Parker's funeral. Congressman Adam Clayton Powell, who pastored the largest church in Harlem, provided a venue so Parker's body could lie in state. Per his mother's request, Charlie's body was returned to Kansas City, Missouri. Charlie's career ran only 14 years, yet he is historically the most commercially successful jazz artist.

A friend of Billie Holiday's, Al Wilde, suggested building a Broadway show around Billie Holiday to create a revenue stream. People in her inner circle liked the concept. Bob Sylvester invested $5,000 in the show. *Holiday on Broadway* ran at the Mansfield Theater on April 27, 1948. The first night sold out. Bobby Tucker accompanied Billie on piano. Other musicians included Slam Stewart and Cozy Cole. Billie changed costumes twice and sang over one dozen tunes. She took five curtain calls after the opening. The New York Times wrote, "Holiday Takes the Evening at Show: Billie, However, Surrounded by Galaxy of Stars of Jazz Work at the Mansfield."[73]

John Levy's club was packed every night with fans flocking through the doors to see Billie Holiday. Ironically, NY police officers did not bother to remove Billie Holiday from the stage at Club Ebony. Bobby Tucker and his group accompanied her. Noro Morales, a Spanish band was on the same bill. John Levy took Billie shopping at high end shops like Florence Lustig's and Wilma. He purchased her $500 gowns with gloves and matching shoes. He gave her jewelry and had her dolled up for shows. John Levy purchased Billie her first mink coat and a matching blue Cadillac. John Levy boasted that he could do more for Billie than Joe Glaser. John Levy even chased Jimmy Monroe off.

Bobby Tucker proposed that even though Billie Holiday was a great jazz singer she harbored a terrible inferiority complex which stemmed from past hurt. On top of the past there was the present and her experience of living.

John booked Billie Holiday at the Strand Theater on Broadway. The Count Basie Band was on the bill too. By then, Billie was earning $3,500 a week, but she did not have any money in her pocket. John Levy controlled her money. He purchased her a home – her first – in St. Albans, Queens, New York. She had her first luxury car and a chauffeur. Her problem with John Levy worsened when he left Billie and the band stranded in the south. Being abandoned with a group of musicians was rough but it was not a deal breaker yet. John controlled her finances. He took care of her needs and controlled her resources. Billie's friends told her they could not understand why her LP's sold for $10 each yet, Billie did not have $10 to go to a restaurant to buy a meal.

In January of 1949, John Levy and Billie Holiday travelled to San Francisco in her Lincoln convertible. The car had a bar in the back and the red leather seat converted into a bed. There was a telephone in her car. In those days doctors were the primary group in society who had phones in their automobiles. John arranged for Billie to perform at Joe Tenner's Café Society Uptown. On the night of January 22, 1949, while the two of them were at Mark Twain Hotel in room 602 at 345 Taylor Street, the telephone rang. Billie answered. A voice asked for John Levy. The caller abruptly hung up.

Then, there was a knock at the door and John handed Billie something and said, "Billie darling, throw this in the toilet[74]." While she was headed to the restroom wearing white silk pajamas, John answered the door and there were three of four white men at the door. One of them tried to pull Billie Holiday away from the toilet. A government expert claimed they found opium in John Levy and Billie Holiday's hotel room and took them to jail and booked them for possession of narcotics. John and Billie were each released from jail on $500 bail. John Levy returned to New York and Billie stayed in San Francisco with physician friends.

The authorities had a weak case on Billie Holiday and John Levy. The arrest report noted that the drug stash was in the wastepaper basket. Agent George White told a reporter that they left the evidence at the scene. Therefore, the police did not have a drug kit as evidence when Billie Holiday and John Levy were booked at the police precinct. Local journalists believed Billie Holiday was being framed.

The following day, *The Oakland Tribute* ran a story on the hotel bust. The headline read "Singer Nabbed On Dope Charge." The story mentioned that Billie Holiday rose to fame after the death of her mentor Bessie Smith, and that she wore her blue mink coat to the police station. The article listed *Strange Fruit* as her signature song. The quote was as follows: "Her recording of "Strange Fruit," the weird, minor key, lament of a Negro lynching has become her virtual trademark[75]."

John Levy was working with the government to help pin drug charges on Billie Holiday. John set up Billie Holiday with his drugs so she could catch another drug case. John confided in Agent Jimmy Fletcher that he wanted to get rid of Billie Holiday because he could not control her. Narcotics Agent Colonel George H. White recalled that Billie Holiday was a drug user and not a drug trafficker which was not normally someone he went after. He felt the government wanted to arrest Billie Holiday because she was flashy. She drove fancy cars, wore fancy coats, and wore fine jewelry and diamonds. But her bandmates felt she had a right to dress and wear what she pleased, and that she was targeted because she used her voice to expose racism.

Agent George White and agents were allegedly corrupt. He often posed as an artist to lure women to his apartment in Greenwich Village. He planted drugs on women. He spiked women's drinks with LSD. Afterward he sexually abused them. After he retired from the bureau he bragged, "Where else could a red-blooded American boy lie, kill, cheat, steal, rape and pillage with sanction and blessing of the All-Highest?[76]" Harry Anslinger wrote in his notes that George could have been high when he busted Billie Holiday because he was a drug user himself.

Billie Holiday insisted that she was not using drugs when they were arrested. Her professional friends suggested Billie check into a facility to allow the doctors to observe her to prove she was not using drugs when the police came in the hotel room. She paid $2,000 to stay at Twin Pines under psychiatric control for four or five days. Billie claimed agents planted drugs on them. She set out to prove her innocence. The doctors observed her and were ready to testify that she was clean. The authorities dropped the charges against John Levy. Billie was not aware that he was a paid informant. Jimmy Fletcher later confirmed John Levy had been an informant since 1934.

The psychologist at Twin Pines, Dr. James Hamilton determined in his recorded interview with Linda Lipnack Huehl that Billie Holiday was a psychopath. He said she was, "an impulse driven, strong, talented, but not dependable individual." She was reckless which got her in trouble. To put it another way, Billie had a drug addiction which is a serious mind-altering illness.

Billie went to trial May 31, 1949. It was not Billie's first rodeo in court. She went to court when she was 10, at 11, when she was 14, when she was in her 20s, when she was 32 and in 1949, when she was 34. Billie Holiday got on the witness stand and admitted she had been in trouble for narcotics before. That day, she told the court she had done her time, society accepted her back and that she was clean. The prosecution argued it did not matter if she was clean or not but what mattered was that she was caught in possession of drugs which violated the law. The jury did not agree with the prosecution and came back and announced, "Not guilty." A crowd of onlookers applauded and cheered loudly. John Levy called Billie after she won the case and congratulated her. Fake!

Billie owed her California lawyer Jake Ehrlich $3,700. He told Billie Holiday he felt sorry for her and that she was a fool because he felt John Levy was using her. One thing was certain, Ehrlich wanted his money. Billie arranged to pay him $500 per week until she paid him in full.

Billie wanted to leave John Levy but reasoned that he had booked shows for her in advance, and she would be sued if she backed out of the shows. So, she stayed with John and tried to have a good relationship with him until she could get untangled from his web. He took grave precautions to control Billie. He had money locked in a safe in the lobby and had paid people to tell him if she went in the safe. He even hid her mink coat under the mattress to make sure she would not go anywhere.

One night, Billie found her mink coat and she left John Levy and returned to New York and checked into a hotel. She was done. She left her first home in Queens, and all its contents. She walked away. At the end of the day, John Levy helped set up Billie Holiday with his drugs. He was working with Harry Anslinger and law enforcement. Attorney Jake Ehrlich saw the writing on the wall. It was time for Billie Holiday to see it.

Meanwhile, she rented another apartment in Harlem and resumed her life anew. She remained popular and was loved especially by youth. Sixteen-year-old Detroit native Lee Walker, known as Bonnie to her friends, William, Ann, Audrey, and Ellen, saw Billie Holiday perform *Strange Fruit* during Spring Break in 1951 at the Apollo Theater. "That night she had on a white outfit, and she had a gardenia in her hair," Bonnie said.

"Back then Spring Break was around Easter. We pooled our money together and drove from Detroit to Harlem to see the performers at the Apollo," Bonnie stated. Like youth do today, they enjoyed popular music and were willing to drive 620 miles for good entertainment.

"When we rode through Pennsylvania, we ran into rainstorms which delayed us. We arrived at the Apollo late," she added. To their surprise the weather was warmer in Harlem. They missed several acts; but they caught Fats Domino, a Rhythm and Blues and Rock and Roll musician and singer. His popular tunes that year were

129

Hey! La Bas Boogie, *She's My Baby*, and *Boogie Woogie Baby*.

A few years later Fats Domino's version of *I Found My Thrill on Blueberry Hill* garnered him national acclaim as a Rock and Roll legend.

I Found My Thrill on Blueberry Hill lyrics.

> I found my thrill
> On Blueberry Hill
> On Blueberry Hill
> When I found you
>
> The moon stood still
> On Blueberry Hill
> And lingered until
> My dream came true
>
> The wind in the willow played
> Love's sweet melody
> But all of those vows you made
> Were never to be[77]

"*Strange Fruit* is my favorite Billie Holiday Song," Bonnie declared, who was 87 years old at the time of the interview. "She had a hard way to go back then," Bonnie said of Billie Holiday. We loved her. Males and females screamed to the top of our lungs when she walked across the stage. "She was graceful and elegant," Bonnie stated.

In those days, girls were wild about Billy Eckstine. He was one of Billie Holiday's favorite singers. Billy Eckstine was tall and handsome. He had cat eyes and a bass-baritone voice. Bonnie and her friends saw him that year in Detroit when he performed at the United Artist Theater at 150 Bagley Street.

Billy Eckstine, New York, N.Y., between 1946 and 1948, by William P. Gottlieb, Library of Congress

"All the girls would scream and jump," Bonnie stated. He always said, 'Steady girls! steady girls!'" Billy Eckstine spoke gently standing in the middle of the stage settling the girls down before he started his show 72 years ago[78].

Billie Holiday got rid of her John Levy heartache. The board was open. It was her move.

Five

The Verve Years

During the Verve years, 1952-1956, the third Billie Holiday period, she recorded four 10" albums and seventeen 12" albums which totaled over 100 songs. Norman Granz became the Record Producer for Clef/Verve Label. He also promoted concerts. Granz returned Billie Holiday's recordings to small groups like her original recordings under the direction of John Hammond in her early Columbia days. Billie Holiday redefined herself during her third period as a torch singer.

Critics argued Billie's voice was weak during her third period due to substance abuse. Others deferred that her distinctive vocal abilities and phrasing prevailed masterfully during her third period. She was charismatic; she made listeners imagine she was singing to them and that the experience of the lyrics was real and present. She was one of the greatest intimate singers of her time.

On Friday, November 14, 1952, Billie Holiday made another Carnegie Hall appearance. She was on the same bill as Duke Ellington, Charlie Parker, Dizzy Gillespie, Stan Getz, and The Ahmad Jamal Trio. There were two shows: one was at 8:30 pm and the other was at 11:45 pm. Concert tickets were $2.40, $3.60, and $4.80. Pianist Memry Midgett accompanied Billie Holiday on stage.

Billie Holiday: Jazz Singer

Flyer announced a Carnegie Hall jazz event 11.14.1952

Memry recalled that Billie was on stage 1 hour and 30 minutes doing encore, after encore, after encore. "Duke Ellington, Sarah Vaughan, Count Basie, Bird, Prez, everyone was there[79]." Memry alleged proudly that the audience was there for one person and that one person was Billie Holiday. Billie was the headliner; she closed the show.

After Billie lost her Cabaret License, she authored articles and sold them to magazines and newspapers as a revenue stream. Although Billie obtained royalties from her Decca records, live shows were lucrative for jazz artists. Not being able to sing in New York clubs hit the pocket of jazz artists deeply. In February of 1953, Billie Holiday authored a story which was published by TAN entitled *Can A Dope Addict Come Back?* By Billie Holiday. She posed for a photograph dressed classy holding two Chihuahuas.

The articles shared bits and pieces of her life story. She shared her perspective about her addiction and recovery. She was raking in funds to support her lifestyle. During the 1950s, even though Billie Holiday sang with jazz bands, she remained misclassified as a blues singer. Jazz musicians backed her vocal performances and recordings.

Her comeback stories attracted the producers of *The Comeback Story,* a television show which sought to encourage people who had fallen in life and were trying to get back on top. Her television appearance, October 2, 1953, entitled, *The Comeback of Billie Holiday, Blues Singer* aired on ABC from 9:30 p.m. to 10:00 p.m. eastern. Her segment was the third production of the show. Billie's voice played in the background. George Jessell, Host, said, "No one who has heard that voice can fail to know its owner. There is only one voice like it. There is only one gal that they call, "Lady Day, The Great Billie Holiday." Jessell asked Billie Holiday to sing *God Bless the Child.*

George Jessell remarked, "The blues ain't nothing but a good woman feeling bad[80]."

Billie Holiday: Jazz Singer

In the audience, in order of appearance, was Charles "Pod" Hollingsworth, Mae Barnes, Artie Shaw, Louis Armstrong, Arthur Herzog Jr. Tallulah Bankhead, and Leonard Feather. Billie's friends and associates read excerpts of her printed magazine and newspapers stories and praised Billie Holiday's musical talent. At the end of the show, George Jessell noted that he and others were hopeful New York would lift Billie Holiday's Cabaret license ban, so Billie could earn a living performing in the jazz clubs in her home State of New York. The event went well.

Not long after Billie broke it off with John Levy, she ran into Louis McKay, who was a mob enforcer, a hustler, and unknown to Billie and her inner circle, he was an informant for NYPD and the feds. She knew him from her teen years when she started singing in Harlem. In 1954, Louis McKay, her business manager, accompanied Billie Holiday on a European tour where she was scheduled to perform 40 concerts including one to two shows per night in Holland, Switzerland, Italy, and France. She had a solo performance in Great Britain. Billie and Louis arrived in Copenhagen on January 10, 1954, greeted by 100s of fans who had flowers, smiles, and cheers.

Billie had the opportunity to talk one on one with fans. She spoke with a doctor and his 12-year-old daughter who told Billie they had listened to every song she ever recorded, and they loved her music. Billie was delighted to meet fans abroad who appreciated her talents. Fans invited Billie to move to Copenhagen. She teasingly noted that she never got that kind of fanfare at LaGuardia Airport.

Billie had a 34-member band backing her concert in London, England. The venue was completely silent as Billie Holiday walked across the stage. All eyes were on

Lady Day. She herself heard the heels of her shoes clinking as she walked to the center of the stage where she had the undivided attention of a massive crowd. The audience applauded whole heartedly. She performed with the same vigor before small as well as large crowds.

Her concert in Brussels, Belgium was recorded live. A trio opened, another followed, then a quartet performed. Billie Holiday closed the show with 10 tunes including *I Cover the Waterfront*, *Willow Weep for Me*, *My Man*, *Lover Come Back to Me*, *Tenderly*, *Them There Eyes*, *Too Marvelous for Words*, *Lover Man*, *Fine and Mellow*, *What a Little Moonlight Can Do*, *Billie's Blues*... Between songs, Billie Holiday paused and conversed with the audience. And at one point she paused and introduced band members and her tune, "Thank you very much. And now I have the pleasure of recording with Benny Goodman, Roy Eldridge, and Teddy Wilson... *What a Little Moonlight*[81]."

Her European tour was a smash. That Summer, John Levy was accused of masterminding an illegal racetrack betting scheme and was arrested in New York. His arrest headlines in *Jet* in the Crime section noted, *Billie Holiday's Ex-Mate Jailed As Bet Ring Kingpin*. John Levy's operation which netted $33,000 per day, was facilitated in Billie Holiday's former home in Queens, New York[82]. John Levy purchased the home with Billie's money in the late 1940s. Billie walked away from her home in 1949 with several suitcases of clothes and jewels and started anew.

As manager, Louis pushed the envelope toward more profits by encouraging Billie to write her autobiography as a means of coming back. She hooked up with her friend William Dufty; she and William co-authored articles and Billie was also a dear friend to his wife, Maely. Billie

Holiday became godmother to their son, Bevan Dufty, born February 27, 1955. She loved him dearly. Billie went to Dufty's place when she was seeking refuge. William collected articles written about Billie Holiday. Then, he interviewed her and started writing her autobiography.

In November of 1955, the final editing for the manuscript *Lady Sings the Blues* by Billie Holiday with William Dufty was ready. The manuscript was written in first person using Billie's voice. The story was told as if readers were having a conversation with Lady Day. The story followed her candid street wise storytelling including her tendency to curse. The editors cleaned the language by replacing the word "bitch" with "whore' and other modifications. The publisher's marketing team felt the candid storytelling with street wise dialogue would sell well. It did. But critics felt the story was too candid. Others loved the book which gave Billie Holiday a new title – author.

On one hand, Billie was street wise and on the other hand the streets proved slippery. In her book, she did not blame anyone for her shortcomings. In real life, she discouraged her musical comrades from using hard drugs. She made it clear she did not want the public to assume her life represented the norm for the Black race. She was proud of singing *Strange Fruit* and being a race woman. Billie Holiday wanted to influence positive improvements in reference to the race issue. True, Billie Holiday told her story because she wanted to make money. Being a convicted felon cost her a lot. She lost her ability to earn money singing in New York's jazz clubs. *Lady Sings the Blues* gave Billie Holiday another wind.

Flyer showing Count Basie and his Orchestra and Lester Young and his Quintet playing at Birdland in 1954.

Billie Holiday wanted the societal race condition to ease the burden it placed on the Black race. She wanted discrimination to go away. She wanted her Cabaret license restored. She wanted and deserved her ability to strive. She wanted Black people of all social classes – maids, butlers, cooks, drivers, singers, musicians, teachers, politicians - to be treated fairly. She had respect for all regardless of one's place in society - straight, crooked, sober, sick, healthy, strong, or weak. Malcolm X certainly said the Black woman was the most unprotected person in America. He said it; he was right.

The Great Lady Day was a prime example that Black women are unprotected. She believed her men would protect her. They did not. They did. She believed her singing talent could sustain her. It had. She was a bastard child in Baltimore. She was Sadie's illegitimate daughter. She was Clarence Holiday's fun child. She wanted to stay out of jail because jail was hell. Every institution where she resided was hell. She was a wayward Black girl at the House of Good Shepherd. She was an inmate at the Federal Women's Reformatory. Harry Anslinger hunted Billie from the moment he sent word for her to cease and desist singing *Strange Fruit* and she refused. Harry felt *Strange Fruit* could incite a race riot because audiences were smitten with Billie Holiday's performance.

How did Harry know? He paid informants to provide written reports on every move Billie Holiday made and who she made each move with.

The KKK or the White Citizen's Council - not much difference either way - asked Rev. George Wesley Lee of Belzoni, Mississippi to cease and desist registering Negro voters in 1955. He refused. He was assassinated gangland style in broad daylight, May 7, 1955, three and a half months before 14-year-old Emmett Till was kidnapped from his family's home in Money, Mississippi, and tortured and murdered August 21, 1955, for allegedly whistling or being fresh – something trivial with Mrs. Carol Bryant. Protesting discrimination and wanting equal rights violated the principles of the White Power Structure in – Southern

America – Northern America – same difference. Billie Holiday was protesting just like her Black brothers and sisters in the south.

Rev. Lee was assassinated for his sins -registering 100 voters. Poor Emmett was tortured and murdered. In New York, Billie Holiday, Charlie Parker, and others were selectively chosen and stripped of their ability to earn a living. A Black person was sitting in the car when white bigots fired their weapons on Rev. Lee. A Black person was on the bed of the truck when Emmett was kidnapped. In New York, Black agents were used to nab Billie Holiday. Agents even planted drugs on Billie. *Strange Fruit* represented in words the imagery of white uncensored gang justice. Tupac Shakur declared in song that the New York police were the biggest gang in America.

The Federal Bureau of Narcotics and the New York Police department ganged up on Billie Holiday. They sent a Black agent and a White agent. They sent two road managers who Billie was deceived to believe where daddies and protectors. The government authorized these men to sell drugs and or use drugs with her. In the drug game, one is either protected or a target. There is a deadend for every target.

Mob justice was the removal of Black men from jails into the public square for a public death without due process of the law. Corruption was corruption – east, west, north, or south. In New York, the police could arrest a Black jazz artist for singing in a club where alcohol was served without his/her Cabaret license. Yet, Frank Sinatra refused to go to the police department and get fingerprinted and photographed to get his Cabaret license and no police officer dared go in any New York club and ask Frank

Billie Holiday: Jazz Singer

Sinatra to show his card. He was Italian. Did the Italian families own New York? Mr. Sinatra or 'Frankie' as Billie fondly called him had Italian privilege. In New York, the Italian mobsters owned the police and more. In, Mississippi, the Klan owned the police and more.

But, but, but, but, musically, Billie Holiday was the Great Lady Day. She became a recording artist at age 18. She was the best. She was great. She was a jazz idol. She was a jazz innovator. She was the queen bee. She became a writer, an author, and an international sensation. No "Dope" headline, no "Jail Again" or "Broke" headline can take Lady Day's fame away from her. Ever!

Billie Holiday told her own story. The 50th Anniversary Edition of *Lady Sings the Blues* was released in 2006. Sure, she fudged a little. Her mother and father never married. Her grandmother had a condition, but Eleanora was not an eyewitness of Mother Fagan's death. But other than that, and her place of birth, she told the truth.

William Dufty was a skilled writer. Eight months top, William typed the manuscript *Lady Sings the Blues* which the acquisition editor was ready to acquire. Louis McKay and Billie Holiday read the manuscript in late 1955. He hired an attorney, Harry A. Lieb, who advised the editors at Doubleday to delete potentially libelous statements in the manuscript. Charles Laughton, actor, Tallulah Bankhead, actor, and John Levy, former lover of Billie's, requested the books reference to them to be omitted in its entirety. She obliged. Like it or not, William Dufty helped Billie Holiday tell her story from her perspective. He knew her well. His house was her second home.

When the book was released in 1956, the *New York*

Herald Tribune wrote of *Lady Sings the Blues* that the book was, "a hard, bitter and unsentimental book, written with brutal honesty and having much to say not only about Billie Holiday, the person, but about what it means to be poor and black in America[83]." Billie acknowledged that she told more but the publisher cut parts of her story.

Ethel Waters' biography *His Eye Is On the Sparrow* was published five years before *Lady Sings the Blues*. Ethel publicly discredited Billie Holiday as a singer, and she certainly had a low opinion of Billie's lifestyle. Ethel and Billie had similar childhoods. Ethel Waters admitted in her biography that she was born out of wedlock, and she grew up Negro and poor; she grew up fast, ran with a gang, and knew about sex by age seven.

Ethel was the product of her 13-year-old mother's rape by her biological father, John Waters, who was a pianist and a playboy. He was poisoned and died when Ethel was three. When Ethel Anderson, the oldest child of Louise Anderson, started singing as a teen, she renamed herself Ethel Waters. Ethel took the only thing she could get from her bloodline – the name. Billie Holiday took her daddy's name too. Ethel told her story. Billie told her story. There was only one Ethel Waters. There was only one Billie Holiday.

After serving time in prison for drugs, Billie was self-conscious; she felt that her haters were waiting for her to fail. They were waiting for her to fail just like her admirers were hoping she would recover from her drug addiction, sing her songs, and walk the straight and narrow. Billie sang a lyric in *He's Funny That Way*, 1937, "But I'm only human, a coward at best." There are ups and downs in life. Billie's ups and downs belonged to her story.

Billie Holiday: Jazz Singer

The publication of *Lady Sing the Blue* and Billie's Tour in Europe were part of her survival as much as it was part of her comeback. On February 10, 1956, Billie Holiday appeared on the Today Show on CBS with Steve Allen. She sang *Please Don't Talk About Me When I'm Gone,* and *I Don't Stand a Ghost of a Chance with You.* During the intermission, Billie promoted her new album *Music for Torching* and her next event at Club Pablo in Washington, D.C.

Thirteen days later, on Thursday, February 23, 1956, Louis McKay and Billie Holiday were arrested in their hotel room for narcotics possession creating more ARREST headlines. That week, Billie Holiday worked at a Showboat in South Philadelphia; then, on Wednesday in the wee hours of the morning she and Louis walked home from the set to their hotel room. Between 2:30 am to 3:00 am the police opened the hotel from the outside, walked in, and showed Louis McKay a warrant.

Louis verified the warrant, asked Billie to put on some clothes, and law enforcement officers ransacked the room looking for narcotics. The toilet bowl was locked immediately so nothing could be flushed down it. A plain clothed female officer searched Billie's body. They found Louis's gun. Louis and Billie were arrested for use and possession of drugs. He was also charged with firearm possession. The police had a card picture file of Louis when he was a juvenile offender. The police gave that picture to the newspaper press.

The detention officers allowed Billie's dog, Pepi, to sleep in her cell. She cuddled Pepi to try to shield her pet from the chilly air in the jail. Billie was bailed out on a $7,500 bond.

She got an advance on her salary to get Louis out of jail. She ate with a few friends from New York in the hotel, got dressed, and went on stage for her first show. In show business, the show must go on. During Billie's performance, the police took one of her accompanists off. They searched him and let him go when they did not find any drugs on him. After Billie finished her second show, Louis was in her dressing room waiting to let her know he had gotten out of jail.

Billie got that monkey off her back. Her doctors told her with any luck she could stay clean for two years. Billie declared, "I've got enough Fagan Irish in me to believe that if the curtains are washed, company never comes. If you expect nothing but trouble, maybe a few happy days will turn up, if you expect happy days, look out[84]."

Sonny Rollins, age 25, and his band were booked on the same bill as Billie Holiday in Newark, New Jersey. They had the opportunity to meet Louis McKay before the gig. "When we were going in the club a white guy was disrespecting Billie Holiday and Louis McKay did not defend her. It was sad to see!" Sonny Rollins declared.

"I have nothing but rotten things to say about Louis McKay. Billie Holiday was at the top of the music business. She was a big star. She was great! I wondered how she ended up with a stiff like Louis McKay[85]," Sonny Rollins stated.

On another occasion, Sonny Rollins played on a bill with Billie Holiday in the Village. Afterward, he got a taxi and took her home to her apartment. He walked her inside, and she gave him an autographed pocket edition of *Lady Sings the Blues*. "Billie Holiday was a beautiful person.

Billie Holiday: Jazz Singer

She was a nice human being," Sonny determined.

That summer, August 13, 1956, Billie appeared on *Stars of Jazz* hosted by Bobby Troup which aired originally on K-ABC-TV Hollywood, Los Angeles, California. She sang *Please Don't Talk About Me When I'm Gone*, *Billie's Blues*, and *My Man*.

"We read it, and we were tremendously impressed. We'll leave the analyzing up to the sociologist," Bobby Troup expressed about Billie's Holiday's new bestselling book, *Lady Sings the Blues*. Billie sang, *It Cost me a Lot But There's One Thing That I've Got it's My Man.* Billie's man and daddy and business manager Louis McKay was in the audience[86].

Bobby Troup was pleased with Billie Holiday's audacity to tell her story. But some were too petty to leave the analysis of Lady Day's story in the hands of sociologists. History has shown us that institutions which are poorly funded and understaffed cause harm to residents, especially minors. *Lady Sings the Blues* does not expose much about the institution for wayward Black girls which was trying to straighten out 10-year-old Eleanora. Her friends noted years later that older girls usually sexually abuse younger girls in group settings. Hurt people try to cure pain with food; others cure pain with substances. When balance is forsaken life falls apart.

An edited recording of the two concerts called *The Essential Billie Holiday: Carnegie Hall Concert Recorded Live* was released. The readings omitted book excerpts about her addiction and events describing racial tensions.

At the end of the evening, Billie Holiday obtained a leather-bound and gold engraved edition of *Lady Sings the Blues* and a plug for the *Coronet* magazine summarization of the book which was on newsstands that day.

Billie Holiday at Carnegie Hall, Nov. 10, 1956. Poster image Courtesy of Carnegie Hall

Billie Holiday: Jazz Singer

Billie Holiday's public and private live crashed after her extraordinarily acclaimed Carnegie Hall concerts. The police followed her every day and sometimes, an officer was at her door warning visitors to stay away from Billie Holiday. She fought back by telling her side of the story to popular and music magazines.

Magazine and news headlines included:

I'll Never Sing with a Dance Band, Billie Holiday, DownBeat

Don't Blame Showbiz!, Billie Holiday, DownBeat

I'm Cured for Good, Ebony

Billie Holiday, Now Remarried, Finds Happiness, A New Sense of Security, DownBeat.

Personally, Billie Holiday did it her way. Musically, she was a genius. She set a new standard for jazz vocalists in 1933. She established herself as a mood singer after she recorded *Strange Fruit* on April 20, 1939. *Strange Fruit* put Billie in the national spotlight rendering her famous at age 23. Listeners could enjoy her music while relaxing. Billie sang the ballads *You Go To My Head*, *Solitude*, *Willow Weep For Me*, and *Do Nothing Til You Hear From Me* beautifully during the Verve years. Billie delivered difficult songs, such as *Prelude to a Kiss,* and *I Don't Want to Cry Anymore* masterfully.

Billie Holiday took charge of recording sessions; she set the moods, keys, and arrangements. She recommended musicians revise specific musical segments. The tunes were replayed until she was satisfied that the melody was coordinated. Like her father, like Prez, and others Billie's musical sense of timing was keen. Like other great musical artists, she simply had a great ear. Basie bandmember Harry (Sweets) Edison described the timeliness of Lester Young's solo, "He didn't put a whole lot of notes in a solo. He put the right note in the right place at the right time... His timing was perfect[87]." Lester Young gave Harry Edison his nickname Sweets.

That winter, on December 9, 1956, Billie Holiday appeared on CBS Radio in Los Angeles, California for *The Greatest Broadcast Ever!* via Woolworth's Jazz Hour with Percy Faith and the Woolworth Orchestra hosted by Donald Wood. Donald Woods said of Billie Holiday, "Certainly a prize exhibit is a gal with a very high-octane talent and a pulsating song personality that adds to the general acoustical joy.[88]" Billie Holiday replied, "Thank you Don. I've got a real song for you now. It's real smoky too. Then Lady Day sang *You Better Go Now* beautifully. She ended the set with *Them There Eyes*.

Excerpts of *Lady Sings the Blues* was narrated by Gilbert Millstein, a New York Times journalist. The piano played during his readings; when he finished the spotlight shined on Billie so she could sing a tune.

Law enforcement dubbed Billie Holiday morally corrupt. Yet, her music inspired listeners. The public purchased her albums, attended her concerts, read her biography, and read magazine articles about her. She was simply loved and admired. Billie Holiday looked her troubles square in the face and then she pulled off another comeback and pressed onward. She continued to make moves in the game called life.

Billie Holiday: Jazz Singer

Six
1957-1959

Billie Holiday and Louis McKay went to Mexico in March of 1957 and got married. The two started dating after Billie's break up with John Levy. Author Robert O'Meally believed Louis used Billie's fame and money to advance himself. Scholars argue Louis asked for Billie's hand in marriage legally so she would not be able to testify against him in a court of law. Louis was a drug dealer who used drugs and collected drug money for New York mobsters and ran his own small, scaled operation and other side hustles. Some argue Billie Holiday was Louis's greatest hustle. In a sense, the mob hustled them both.

Aside from those views, Billie Holiday was known as the Queen Bee in jazz and as the Great Lady Day.

Louis hit Billie like he was hitting a man he was collecting drug money from. Friends noted that Louis knocked her out cold more than once and let her lay on the floor and sleep off her intoxication. He prostituted a string of women whom he often physically abused. People in the music industry called Billie Holiday Louis McKay's stage prostitute. She was trying to make it from one gig and one day to the next. Her life was hard. Yet, she kissed her music and reigned on the stage.

Author Johann Hari of *Chasing the Scream* discovered documents which verified that Louis McKay was an informant on Anslinger's payroll. According to his findings, Louis agreed to help Anslinger's staff set up Billie Holiday in 1947. Louis McKay was careless with her money as a business manager. After he lost a great deal of her money in a risky business deal, Billie was devastated.

Eventually, Louis broke Billie's trust and one day she told a friend she physically got the best of him and stuck his head in the commode. Shortly after that, she was done. He moved to California where he had already purchased property in his name with Billie's money. He planned to have his ducks in a row. Billie did not go to the police. She did not have any friends at the police station; she did not trust law enforcement.

Like Prez who drank his pain away, Billie drank and indulged in heavy drug usage to kill her pain. Prez never did hard drugs. Substance cannot kill mental pain and anguish. Substance abuse creates problems on top of problems.

After parting ways with Louis, Billie moved into an apartment in Harlem. Living alone with her dog was lonely. Her wealth had flown east and west with a flock of birds following Joe Guy, John Levy, and Louis McKay. She was starting again in one sense. John Levy was still using the beautiful large roomy house he bought in the Queens with her money. By 1958, Billie was sick. Her pain was intense. Her ankles were often swollen. She had been betrayed too many times to count. Her spirit was wounded.

Her friends encouraged her and helped her get from one point to another toward another come back. Unfortunately, her health was declining, and she indulged more in substances. Her friends and accompanists risked their freedom scoring drugs for Billie Holiday. She was followed day and night; she could not walk to a drug house and score anything.

She doctored her pain with substances. Her friends helped her put one foot in front of the other. They did whatever was necessary to help hold her up. That's what friends do. God bless devoted friends. Some people only get three devoted friends in their entire lives. If one beats the three in a lifetime ratio, he or she has beaten the odds. If you beat the odds, count your blessings. Loyalty is priceless.

Billie had to work to put bacon and ribs on the table. Her best earning years had passed. Saturday, July 6, 1957, Billie performed at the Newport Jazz Festival, in Newport County, Rhode Island, which was not her best day. Billie's voice was not up to par; she stumbled over lyrics she had sung hundreds of times. But the pianist smoothed over her voice stumbles, and the audience gave Lady Day a healthy applause. Everyone has a dreadful day. Billie was having a rough season. She had lost body weight. She was frail and experiencing physical pain. Her liver was declining. Her daddy's (men, lovers, managers, husbands) had failed her. Yet she pressed on.

The Newport Jazz Festival, Thursday, July 4, 1957, lineup included:

Ella Fitzgerald	George Lewis Band
Henry (Red) Allen	Jack Teagarden
Kid Ory	Louis Armstrong & His All-Stars
Sidney Bechet	

The Newport Jazz Festival, Friday, July 5, 1957, lineup included:

Bobby Hackett
Cannonball Adderley
Errol Garner Trio
Mat Mathews
The Bernard Peiffer Trio
Stan Kenton and His Orchestra

The George Shearing Quintet
Carmen McRae
Gigi Gryce
Ruby Braff

The Newport Jazz Festival, Saturday, July 6, 1957, lineup included:

Billie Holiday
Cecil Taylor Quartet
Chris Connor
Sonny Stitt Quartet
Don Eliott Quartet
Gerry Mulligan Quartet
Jimmy Smit Trio

Rolf Kuhn
Dave Brubeck Quartet
Horace Silver Quintet
Eddie Costa
Jackie Paris
Kai Winding
Dizzy Gillespie & His Orchestra

The Newport Jazz Festival, Sunday, July 7, 1957, lineup included:

Jimmy Rushing
Sarah Vaughan
Teddy Wilson Trio
Oscar Peterson Trio

Count Basie and His Orchestra
Stuff Smith
Jimmy Giuffre 3
Wilbur de Paris

During the winter of 1957, December 8, 1957, Billie recorded *Fine and Mellow* on *The Sound of Jazz*, a one-hour television special, Sunday evening on CBS. *The Sound of Jazz* was part of *The Seven Lively Arts* television series. It was the first major television production about jazz on the American Television Network. The lineup included Lester Young, Ben Webster, Coleman Hawkins, Gerry Mulligan (saxophonists); Roy Eldridge and Doc Cheatham (trumpets); Vic Dickerson (trombone); Mal Waldron (piano); Danny Barker (guitar); Milt Hinton (bass); and Osie Johnson (drums).

Lady Day and Prez on the Sound of Jazz – 1957. Courtesy of the NY Public Library.

The musicians were smoking and talking when they were not playing. Billie Holiday walked through happily and playfully joking with members of the Count Basie band who she had known for years. She sat on a high stool and sang. As Billie started singing, the musicians helped Lester stand on his feet so he could play beautifully while Billie sang as he had many times.

Before the television recording, Lester Young and Billie Holiday's relationship was estranged. Yet, onlookers became emotional watching Lester and Billie stare deeply into each other's eyes across the room from each other as he played his saxophone, and she sang. Their deep trance took them to a place and time that only Billie and Lester had gone.

Billie knew things about Lester. Lester knew things about Billie. Billie knew Lester had been court-martialed for possession and use of marijuana when he was in the Army during WWII at a base in Ft. McClellan, Alabama and that his detention was traumatic because drunken, loud, hateful, and evil white guards terrorized Lester. He was punished and required to perform hard labor.

Lester knew about her trauma and that it started when she was an innocent child. Lester drank heavily for the rest of his life. Across the room, she saw his feebleness. He had changed. She had changed. The face had changed. The steadiness had changed. The grip had changed. The process of life had taken a turn for him and for her. Racism, sexism, exploitation, and coping collided. Bomb!

During the solo, it was obvious Lester was sick because he had to gather his strength while the band played *Fine and Mellow*. Lester told a reporter after the set that Lady Day was still his girl, and she was still the best. Historically, from 1937 to 1946, Billie Holiday and Lester Young recorded 60 songs together.

Billie Holiday: Jazz Singer

Professionally, Billie Holiday was hanging in there as best as she could. Personally, Billie Holiday's relationships consistently fell apart; no one was loyal - husband and wife, lover, neither she nor them were devoted to one another. The powerful mobsters had Harry Anslinger in their pockets and Harry had Jimmy Fletcher, John Levy and Louis McKay on his payroll. The pusher man had all the profits in their pockets. This tip of balance against Billie Holiday was destructive. Billie Holiday ate off the same plate with her enemies and slept in the bed with her enemies. She kept breathing. Yes. But!

The government had a grip on Billie Holiday's demise. The government effectively had three men up close and personal infiltrate Billie's private life. Agent Jimmy Fletcher entered Billie's inner circle as a fan and was part of the first sting to raid her hotel room in 1947. John Levy, Billie's lover and manager, set her up for a sting in a California hotel in 1949. John told her to get rid of his opium after he received a phone call that Law Enforcement was on the way up to conduct the bust.

After one of John Levy's beatings, Billie's friends, Bobby Tucker, and Buck Clayton had to tape her ribs before she got on stage to sing at a gig. The extreme pain from broken ribs is excruciating. It takes a long time to heal fractured bones. Being ruthlessly beaten was disturbing.

Billie's friends recalled that John kicked Billie, but he never hit her in the face. He wanted her to be able to perform on stage. Billie made money singing on stage. Finally, in the end, there was Louis McKay, a handsome devil, he was.

That December day in the CBS studio, Billie was looking at Prez across the room blowing his saxophone. She saw him. She saw herself. He had declined. He had changed. She had declined. She had changed. Life had taken a turn. Prez and Lady Day gave those moments in music the best they had to give.

Billie figured out how to get new liftoffs. Norman Granz was ready to deliver. When she met Norman in the early 1940s, he was a college student at UCLA. Now he was Verve Record's Artistic Director. He used top musicians such as, the pianists, Jimmy Rowles, Bobby Tucker, Wynton Kelly; horn players Ben Webster, Benny Carter, Coleman Hawkins, Budd Johnson, Flip Philips, Willie Smith, and Paul Quinichette; and Trumpet players Harry "Sweets" Edison, Charlie Shavers, or Joe Newman in 1958 to reissue Billie Holiday's album *Stay With Me*.

Although Billie Holiday's health was declining, Robert O'Meally proposed that Billie's Verve recordings *I Didn't Know What Time It Was*, *Our Love is Here to Stay*, and *We'll Be Together Again* matched in quality the Holiday-Young recording from the 1930s in her hay day.

Billie's voice and technique matured. She had 'it.' She used 'it.'

Although pleased with the Verve recordings, Lady Day did not renew her contract with Verve and resigned to Columbia hoping to have a production similar in quality to a recording arranged for Frank Sinatra in 1950. The deal came into fruition. In 1958, Columbia recorded Billie Holiday's *Lady in Satin* album which was her most expensive recording production. There were three female background singers, a full string section, and a big band featuring the nation's best jazz and classical musicians.

Billie Holiday: Jazz Singer

During the *Lady in Satin* production, Billie's health and vitality worsened; record producers were frustrated with her work ethic. The recording session was scheduled to start at 10 pm; yet Billie arrived at 12 midnight. Even though she had to be assisted in her seat for recording sessions, and missed some lines, her phrasing and emphasis went well. The musicians noted that even with her health issues Billie was not a sad sack. She joked around and laughed like the old days.

Her arranger was frustrated. He was fed up with too many late starts and retakes. On the set, she was drinking gin from a water pitcher. However, the musicians were pleased and in their eyes Billy Holiday – Lady Day was still a star. Billy Holiday did not desire the backup singers. But she loved her new song list such as *Violets for Your Furs* and *You've Changed*. She cried while singing *You've Changed*. Yes sir. A lot had changed. She was estranged from her husband Louis McKay. He went from protecting her to being a monster she needed protection from.

Though she had tried 100 times to beat that horse. She was back on the wagon. She had once had the strength of a beast and now she needed basic living assistance. Lady Day was not a victim. She said so herself. She lived life her way. She did it the Billie Holiday way. She invented Billie Holiday. Her friends risked their freedom getting drugs for her to help her get well when she was going through withdrawals. Not all schemed off the top. Sometimes, funds were too low for an extra cut. She had her voice. She used it.

Music critics found fault in the *Lady in Satin* album. Critics argued the album signaled Billie Holiday's departure from the jazz genre into pop. Miles Davis said, "I'd rather hear her now. She's become much more mature. Sometimes you can sing words every night for five years, and all of a sudden it dawns on you what the song means[89]."

Billie Holiday's article, *I Needed Heroin to Live,* published by *Confidential* in October of 1958, was co-written by William Dufty. She was paid $1,500 for the article[90]. By then, she was suffering with liver problems and drinking an alcohol cocktail for breakfast every morning and drinking from sunup to sundown.

In an interview with Chris Alberton on August 24, 1958, for WCAU-FM radio in Philadelphia, Lester Young was asked to name his favorite singers. Lester dubbed Jo Stafford and Lady Day his favorite singers. After he mentioned those two names, he added, "And I'm through[91]." Lester highlighted that he could hear Jo Stafford's voice. In other words, the singer's ability to articulate the lyrics clearly to listeners was significant.

Billie used her voice as if it was a horn, and Lester made the sounds coming from his saxophone sound like a voice. She was careful which words and phrases she emphasized. Lester never played every note; but he emphasized the rights notes.

Lester Young was the son of Willis Lester Young, a school principal, a trumpeter, a band leader, and leader of a vaudeville show. Willis tried to keep his children close so he could protect them. He did not allow his daughter to be a maid because Negro female domestic workers including girls were often sexually abused and raped at a whim by southern white males particularly. Willis wanted his sons to follow the southern customs for Negro entertainers, but Lester felt the old norms were a drag. After travelling to

Billie Holiday: Jazz Singer

Kansas and to New Jersey and New York, Lester discovered that racism was – beyond the south – country deep.

Both Lester and Billie adopted negative coping measures to cradle their pain. It was their choice. In the meantime, they fed their musical genius, which was absolutely the opposite of negative which was positive which was greatness which is Lady Day and Prez all day long without a single doubt.

On October 3, 1958, Billie Holiday, Mal Waldron, Bennie Carter, Buddy DeFranco, and Gerry Mulligan performed at the 1st Annual Monterey Jazz Festival in Monterey, California. Her show won multiple encores from the audience. Her voice went over well, and the band played beautifully. Louis Armstrong, Dizzy Gillespie, Max Roach, and Sonny Rollins were there. Today, the Monterey Jazz Festival is the longest continuous jazz festival in the world.

Billie had amazing friends. Alice Vrbsky shopped for Billie and took her clothes to the cleaners. Frankie Freedom ran errands for Billie. He even cleaned and sanitized her needles. Annie Ross fixed Billie's hair when she was in town. Billie Holiday kept maintaining. She kept singing.

Billie Holiday appeared at the Apollo Theater February 23, 1959, and she sang *Please Don't Talk About Me When I'm Gone*. Her hair was slicked back, and she was wearing a long ponytail. She swung her arms to the rhythm of the beat holding her thumb and index fingers close, but she never popped her fingers. She appeared incredibly pleased with the crowd. Of the 100s of songs in her list it was interesting that she sang *Please Don't Talk About Me When I'm Gone* twice that month.

Please Don't Talk About Me When I'm Gone lyrics

Please don't talk about me when I'm gone
Honey, though our friendship ceases from now on
And if you can't say anything real nice
It's better not to talk at all, is my advice

We're parting, you'll go your way, I'll go mine
I have just this to do
Give a little kiss and hope that it brings
Lots of love to you
Makes no difference how I carry on (but I'll make It, baby!)
Please don't talk about me when I'm gone...[92]

Written by Bee Palmer, Sidney Clare, and Sam Stept

Billie Holiday's last recording session was divided into three ensembles. Two ensembles included strings and one without strings. There were three soloists: Trombonist Jimmy Cleveland, Trumpetist Harry "Sweets" Edison, and Alto Saxophonist Gene Quill. Sweets, a former member of the Count Basie Band, played trumpet for her Verve recording in 1957 and had played previously with Lady and Prez many times since 1937.

Sweets also played on Frank Sinatra recordings. Billie sang several songs for the first time including *All The Way*, *I'll Never Smile Again* – Sinatra previously recorded both songs. She also sang *There'll Be Some Changes Made*, which was a former Ethel Waters's hit. Billie recorded one Bessie Smith song - *Baby, Won't You Please Come Home*. Billie also sang a new song *It's Not for Me to Say*. During the recording Billie Holiday was frail. Occasionally, Billie's housekeeper, secretary, Alice Vrbsky, had to hold Billie up

Billie Holiday: Jazz Singer

in the chair. Alice paused the recording when she felt Billie needed to rest. Most recordings were first takes. Some songs were faded at the end of the recording which meant Billie could not hold the last note. The original title *Billie Holiday* was changed to *Last Recording*. It was released in December of 1959.

Sunday, March 15, 1959, the great tenor saxophonist Lester "Prez" Young died in New York. Days later at his funeral Billie told several friends she was next. Billie took Lester's death hard. She was frail; she was drinking a lot, eating less, and losing weight. After Lester died, Elaine Swayne, who had allegedly been Lester's live-in girlfriend before his death, visited Billie, and the two discussed Lester. According to one source, Billie was touched that Lester had someone who was there for him when he was sick; she was sick; she did not have a mate. However, one of Lester's bandmates determined Lester moved into the hotel because he was sick, and he did not want to burden his family.

Lester Young toured Europe during the winter of 1959. On February 6, 1959, a month before his death, **Lester was interviewed by a jazz journalist** François Postif in Paris, Francis. Lester expressed his deep distain of the discriminatory practices Black people faced in the jazz industry and in the United States of America.

Lester said, "I just can't take that bullshit! You dig it? It's all bullshit. And they want everybody who is a Negro to be an Uncle Tom, and Uncle Remus, or Uncle Sam. And I can't make it."

Lester added, "All I can do is tell you what happened."

Finally, Lester told François, "It's the same way all over. You dig? You just fight for your life. That's all. Until death do, we part. You got it made[93]."

His last two recording sessions were completed March 7, 1959, in Paris. During the recording, he was ill; he had a poor appetite during his European tour. Reportedly, he drank a fifth of alcohol every day for 20 years.

At his funeral Lester's wife, Mary Berkeley Young, did not allow Billie to sing because Mary felt Billie looked too sick and frail. Billie was heartbroken that she could not pay a tribute in song to Prez. She broke down and cried. Buck Clayton, Teddy Wilson, and others helped Billie walk outside. They took her to a bar next door and bought her a drink. She calmed down. But she regretted losing control of her emotions at the funeral. You know how it goes – *never let em' see you sweat*.

Billie Holiday's brother by another mother was an influential jazz artist, who stepped on the jazz scene after Louis Armstrong and preceded Charlie Parker. Charlie Parker, known in the jazz world as 'Bird' was influenced by Prez. Charlie had greater commercial success. Charlie modeled his style from Prez.

Tenor Saxophonist Sonny Rollins who was influenced by Coleman Hawkins declared of Lester Young, "He was a god.[94]"

Sonny Rollins said in an interview that a friend on his block in Harlem knew he was a Coleman Hawkins fan and he asked Sonny, "Who is the greatest tenor man? Sonny replied, "Coleman Hawkins," who was his idol.
The young man disputed Sonny and declared Lester

Billie Holiday: Jazz Singer

Young the greatest tenor saxophonist. Sonny had never heard Lester play; so, he made it his business to check Lester out. Sonny discovered that Lester Young was a musical genius. From the moment Sonny discovered the sound of Lester Young, he was in awe of Lester just like he was of Coleman Hawkins. The first Lester Young recording Sonny purchased was *Sometimes I'm Happy*. Sonny said, "Boy it was just fantastic." After that Sonny purchased every Lester Young recording and like Charlie Parker, Sonny became a Lester Young student. Sonny, age 14, recalled playing *Three Little Words*[95] in 1944 every night featuring Lester Young and friends: Bill Coleman, trumpet, Dicky Wells, trombone, Joe Bushkin, piano, John Simmons, bass, and Jo Jones, drums.

Sonny Rollins recalled that Lester Young was open and warm to local youth. "We used to walk to Lester Young's apartment. He used to tell us his life story[96]," Sonny Rollins said.

Scholars dubbed Lester Young a creative poet and trendsetter. Lester was the first person to use the term 'cool' to associate it with a state of mind. When Lester said, "I'm cool," he meant I am calm and or I am okay with the plan. Lester was original. When invited to play a gig, Lester often asked, "What does the bread smell like?" He was the first person to popularize using the word 'bread' to refer to money.

When someone insulted Lester, he pulled out a small whisk broom and brushed off his shoulder which reminds one of Jay-Z brushing off his shoulder with his hand when he sang his hit single *Dust Off Your Shoulders* in 2009. Even the first Black President Barack Obama publicly brushed off his shoulders. When a bigot walked in their space, Lester said, "I feel a draft." He rang a little bell when a musician made a mistake on the bandstand. His father, Willis Young, hit his children with a leather strap when they made musical mistakes.

Lester Young's advice was "You gotta' be original, man![97]" Billie Holiday was original. When she was a teenager, she refused to change her style of singing slow for audiences. She did not try to imitate Ethels Waters. She created the Billie Holiday sound. Lester named her Lady Day, and she named him Prez. Every time there was a shift in jazz from Swing to Bebop, Billie Holiday revised her song repertoire. She did not care to sing a song the same way twice. The musicians in the Count Basie Band only earned $14 per week in the 1930s. Later in life, Lester Young was rewarded for his jazz genius. He earned $50,000 per year in the 1950s until his death on March 15, 1959.

Lester's saxophone style rendered him the father of the 'cool school' of jazz which Miles Davis and others popularized. Lester was Billie Holiday's favorite musician. Lester Young recorded with the Count Basie Orchestra and Billie Holiday in the 1930s and 1940s. His saxophone complimented some of Billie Holiday's best recordings including *He's Funny That Way, Travin' All Alone*, and *Easy Livin.'*

Billie Holiday bragged on Prez, "… he could blow 15 choruses in a row. Each one prettier than the last.[98]"

Lester's revolutionary style hit the New York scene in 1934. His saxophone sounded like a vibrato-less tenor which was fast, airy, clean, and light. Dizzy Gillespie called Lester's sound a "cool flowing style[99]." Lester Young played long phrases with strategic use of silence and

Billie Holiday: Jazz Singer

space and rhythmic mastery. Lester influenced 100s of musicians. Lester Young and Billie Holiday were both hipsters who influenced jazz culture, Black cultural pride, and they broke racial barriers through music.

Billie was glamorous and hip; she popularized calling men daddy. By the 1960s and 1970s, the words 'daddy' and 'daddio' were mainstream in Black culture. Lester called his old girlfriends "a wayback." He referred to police officers in conversation as "Bing and Bob." Lester was the first jazz musician to wear sunglasses on stage. He wore a pork-pie hat. Billie wore her gardenias in her hair.

Lester Prez Young was buried at The Evergreens Cemetery at 1629 Bushwick Avenue, Brooklyn, NY. By Scott Stanton

On March 15, 1959, Billie Holiday was troubled by Lester's passing; she envisioned her own passing; she tried to keep herself going. On April 7, 1959, she threw a 44th Birthday party for herself in her "garden apartment" at 26 W. 87th Street off Columbus Avenue. She prepared fish stuffed with hamburger and peppers, salad, greens, and black-eyed peas. In the old days, Sadie used to cook and wait on Billie's friends.

Leonard Feather felt Billie looked sickly, and he suggested she check herself in a hospital to rest. She told Leonard she was not going to a hospital because she did not trust the hospital staff. Friends said Billie did not want to go to a hospital because she could not get heroin easily. She needed medical treatment or heroin to stay alive if she was back on that horse.

The April 24, 1959, lynching of 23-year-old Mack Charles Parker, a Black man accused of raping a pregnant White lady spurred a national outcry. The horrific fate of Mack Charles Parker was world news. None of the white men who abducted Mr. Parker from his jail cell before his jury trial and lynched him were indicted or arrested. Mack Charles Parker was the lifeless 'strange fruit' near Poplarville, Mississippi which Billie Holiday started singing about in 1938. *No justice, no peace*. Mercy!

May 25, 1959, Leonard Feather booked Billie Holiday to perform a benefit concert, at the Phoenix Theater in Greenwich Village. Billie arrived early to get dressed and put on make-up. By then she was visibly frailer and according to Comedian Steve Allen who was there when she arrived, Billie looked twice her age. Steve recalled that she had gone from a healthy-looking woman, 50 pounds heavier, to a frail much older looking woman. Steve noted that he and Leonard helped Billie get on stage to the mic. He said she sounded terrible. Leonard recalled later to an interviewer that he had to fight his tears when he saw her.

She was drinking a quart of gin every day and smoking Pall Malls heavily. By then, she started drinking as soon as her feet hit the floor. She had a poor appetite, but Billie was always professional; she cared deeply about singing, her public appearance, her fans, and earning money.

Six days after the benefit concert, May 31, 1959, Billie Holiday collapsed in her apartment. Her friend sent her to Knickerbocker Hospital. She was signed in the hospital as Eleanora McKay. The medical staff did not know she was the famous Singer Lady Day. She was regarded as a throw a-way junkie riddled with needle marks. So, she was in the hall untreated for hours. Plus, Knickerbocker Hospital did not provide methadone treatments to drug addicts. A Viennese doctor who was a fan of Billie Holiday arranged her transfer to Metropolitan Hospital in Harlem so she could receive medical treatment.

During Billie's 47-day hospital stay, her lawyer advised her to sign a contract to obtain a new agent authorizing the agent to find a film which would feature Billie, to produce magazine articles, and the authority to draft a new book called *Bless My Bones*. At the time of these new developments, Joe Glaser was her agent, and he was paying her bills. Joe Glaser purchased a plane ticket for Louis McKay, who was legally Billie's husband, to come help. The hospital staff was only allowing family and the press to enter her room. Louis arrived from California with a contract too. He asked Billie to sign the rights of *Lady Sings the Blues* to him. She pretended to be too ill to understand his request and refused to sign the contract.

Billie was in an oxygen tent fighting to live; yet death was fighting to take over. The hospital had strict visitation rules which were ridiculous. Anyone who loves a person should be able to visit someone who is critically ill. The Dufty's and other people contacted Billie Holiday when she was terminally ill: Leonard Feather, Alice Vrbsky, Detroit Red, Louis McKay's sister Kay Kelly, Joe Glaser, Francis Church (Glaser's assistant), lawyers, and a few others. Frank Sinatra visited. Other friends sent flowers to her room. A hospital Roman Catholic Church chaplain administered her last rites.

One day a nurse alleged she found drugs in Billie Holiday's room and reported the drugs to the police. At that very hour, Billie was being fed intravenously and receiving blood transfusions. Maely Dufty believed there was no way Billie Holiday had the strength to use the heroin which the nurse found in a piece of foil six feet away from the bottom of her hospital bed. She had equipment strapped to her legs and arms for the transfusion; so, it was impossible for her to reach the substance let alone inject it.

The police arrested Billie Holiday in her hospital bed Friday, June 12, 1959, and put her under 24-hour police guard placing two officers at her doorless room. Then, she was hand cuffed to her hospital bed; she was fingerprinted, and her mugshot was photographed while she was in her hospital bed. The police took away her radio, her *Confidential* magazines, her record player, her comic books, her flowers, cards, and everything from a woman dying from cirrhosis of the liver and other complications. Prior to her arrest, she was receiving methadone treatments and showing signs of improving. Law enforcement told doctors to stop her methadone treatments, although, she had picked up weight and her health had improved. The authorities removed Billie Holiday from the critical list to hasten her demise.

The government used the photos to show the public that the War on Drugs had nabbed a big fish. In reality, the big fish were collecting big money from the drug trade. Small fish were paying the price in jail time, lost wages, and the physical cost of using drugs. Law enforcement were the heroes rather than leaders who ran racist and inhuman operations. Nothing can be more inhuman than arresting a woman receiving blood transfusions and removing her from the critical list to hasten her demise.

Other eyewitnesses agreed with Maely that Billie could not sit up without physical assistance. She was too weak to have reached up and places drugs where the drugs were hidden. William Dufty called the mayor and other politicians and tried to get them to intervene and stop the police from placing so many indignities on a woman on her death bed.

An hour before she passed, she told the nurse to take a roll of cash $750.00 (rolled like a cigarette) and give it to Bill. She had earned the money from *Confidential*. William (Bill) Dufty wrote the piece to get quick cash for Billie Holiday. *Confidential* paid Billie Holiday $840.00 for the article. William gave Billie the money; she kept $750 and gave him $90 for his troubles. When the nurse found William Dufty and gave him the money, he knew immediately that Billie Holiday was dying and there was nothing he or anyone could do about it. Billie Holiday died with a small cash reserve. But her royalties at the end of 1959 totaled over $100,000.

Dufty recalled during Billie Holiday's last moments, she

was sleeping, breathing hard, and struggling for air. She was fighting for her life. The Angel of Death was hovering over Billie. The nurse felt her pulse and announced, "She's gone.[100]" Billie was pronounced dead at 3:30 a.m. The official cause of death was serious heart, kidney, and liver ailments that were fatally complicated by a lung blockage.

When Billie Holiday died, Frank Sinatra stayed in his New York penthouse for two days, weeping, drinking, and playing Billie Holiday records. In 1944, Billie Holiday told Columnist Earl Wilson she offered Sinatra advice on his singing. "I told him certain notes at the end he could bend. Bending those notes – that's all I helped Frankie with."

To her that shared wisdom was a little, bitty insignificant thing. But Frank Sinatra felt her advice was monumental. He said in 1958, "It is Billie Holiday… who was, and still remains, the greatest single musical influence on me[101]."

Lady Day's body was handled by Universal Funeral Home on 52nd and Lexington Avenue. She was funeralized Tuesday, July 21, 1959, at St. Paul the Apostle Church on 16th Street at Ninth Avenue in New York. Billie Holiday was laid to rest in her favorite pink laced stage gown and gloves. During her public viewing, Louis McKay kneeled in front of Lady Day's casket wearing black shades. At her graveside were William Dufty, Maely Dufty, Joe Glaser, Little Jimmy Scott, Benny Goodman, Gene Krupa, Tony Scott, and Buddy Rogers; others attended her funeral along with 3,000 fans. Benny Goodman was one of her honorary pallbearers. Five hundred people stood outside the church.

Maely Dufty spoke adamantly against law enforcement

blaming narcotic police for murdering Billie Holiday. Police presence was very visible at Billie Holiday's funeral because law enforcement feared a riot would break out.

The day of her funeral, the jazz musicians did not gather at a watering hole nearby to give Lady Day a New Orleans styled toast to celebrate the life of someone who just transitioned from earth. They were too sad to keep customs. They went home to mourn another great loss in the jazz world. The jazz world lost Lester Young March 15, 1959, and Billie Holiday on July 17, 1959. Fellow musicians, bandmates, and loved ones remembered those dates for the rest of their lives on earth.

St. Paul the Apostle Church, July 21, 1959. Streetview of Billie Holiday's funeral. New York Public Library

Meredith Coleman McGee

Seven
Aftermath

Billie Holiday filed for divorce from Louis McKay before she passed, but it was never finalized. She avoided signing over the rights of *Lady Sings the Blues* to Louis McKay when she was on her death bed. However, since she died without a will, under New York law, Louis obtained the royalties to her book, royalties to her recordings, and the rights to her intellectual property and image anyway. Though urged by her lawyer to write a will, she felt writing a will was bad luck, and never wrote one. Listen to the lyrics of *My Man*. You will hear Billie Holiday singing, "I'm his forevermore." How ironic her decision not to write a last will and testament gave her estate to her estranged husband who helped the government destroy her.

The jazz world lost Lester Young and Billie Holiday in 1959. On the international front, 1959 was the year, Fidel Castro rose to power in Cuba after the country's revolution. Alaska was admitted as the 49th U.S.A. state. Hawaii became the 50th state. Berry Gordy Jr. formed Motown Records in January of 1959 at 2648 West Grand Boulevard in a two-story house in Detroit, Michigan.

Café Society vanished. Billie Holiday vanished. But *Strange Fruit* imprinted the racial injustice banner deep in the hearts and souls of men. Today, one can hear Billie Holiday sing *Strange Fruit* and hear Nina Simone's version

Billie Holiday: Jazz Singer

of *Strange Fruit* on wax, on CD, on Disc, on Spotify...

Billie Holiday's Cabaret License was never renewed. She could not sing in any club in NYC. But she was a jazz icon to the end. She performed 22 times, from 1948 to 1958, at Carnegie Hall, the largest and most prestigious venue in the city.

Change was difficult. Change was inevitable. Jazz changed in 1959. Jazz exploded commercially. That was the year Miles Davis released *Kind of Blue,* a masterpiece which sold 5 million copies and it provided the blueprint for modern jazz. It became the best-selling jazz album in history. *Kind of Blue* was rated the best-selling album in any musical genre. Like Billie Holiday, jazz musicians demanded respect. They did not want the cash register to ring during their performances. Billie Holiday's former neighbor, Miles Davis demanded reverence from audiences for his art too.

Kind of Blue featured Miles Davis on trumpet and John Coltrane on saxophone. The rhythm section contained Paul Chambers, Jimmy Cobb, and Wynton Kelly. The three players included Julian Cannonball Adderley, Jimmie Cobb, and Bill Evans.

That year, the Dave Brubeck Quartet, a white group, also broke records and gained significant commercial success with the release of the jazz album *Time Out*. The quartet's single *Take Five* became the highest selling jazz single on a 45 ever recorded. Negroes started jazz. However, in 1959, jazz exploded in white America and internationally.

In 1961, Black people excelled in a variety of music genres. Ray Charles won four grammy awards... *The*

Meredith Coleman McGee

Genius of Ray Charles, *Let the Good Times Roll*, *Georgia on My Mind*. Leontyne Price won Best Classical Performance -Vocal Soloist. Harry Belafonte won Best Performance – Folk for *Swing Dat Hammer*. Two white jazz artists won jazz grammy awards. Andre Previn won Best Jazz Performance Solo or Small Group for *West Side Story*. Henry Mancini won Best Jazz Performance Large Group for *Blues and the Beat*.

Gil Evans, a white, Canadian American pianist and composer and Miles Davis won Best Jazz Composition of More Than Five Minutes Duration for *Sketches of Spain*. Ella Fitzgerald won Best Vocal Performance Single Record or Track, Female for *Mack the Knife*. And she won Best Vocal Performance Album, Female for *Mack the Knife – Ella in Berlin*. Count Basie won Best Performance by a Band for Dancing for *Dance Along with Basie*.

After the state of New York settled the affairs of Eleanor Fagan McKay, known as Billie Holiday, Louis McKay collected royalties from her music and intellectual property sales throughout the 1960s and 70s. He earned consultant fees for the 1972 movie *Lady Sings the Blues* produced by Motown Productions and Paramount Pictures. Diana Ross and Billy Dee Williams were remarkable in the film. She played Billie Holiday; he played Louis McKay. Louis McKay was the first Black booking agent in Hollywood, California.

According to one account, Joe Glaser tried to obtain the rights to Billie Holiday's book *Lady Sings the Blues*. However, New York law was on the side of the surviving spouse – Louis McKay.

The year after Billie Holiday's death President John F. Kennedy honored Harry Anslinger for his War of Drugs.

Billie Holiday: Jazz Singer

Harry Anslinger retired in 1962. He served as Commissioner of the U.S. Bureau of Narcotics for 32 years.

1961 Newport Music Festival poster. Carmen McRae, Billie Holiday mentee, song on the same bill with Louis Armstrong.

Joe Guy, Billie's former boyfriend and business manager,

born September 29, 1920, died young too, at age 41, on June 1, 1962, in Birmingham, Jefferson County, Alabama. He was laid to rest at Shadowlawn Memorial Park.

Dinah Washington had a short but fulfilling musical career. She sang jazz, blues, R&B, and gospel. She died in 1963 in Detroit, Michigan at age 39.

In 1966, Leonard Feather released an Encyclopedia of Jazz Vol. One the Blues. Verve[102].

Actress Judy Garland, a fan and friend of Billie Holiday, died at age 47, June 23, 1969, in London, England by an accidental overdose of barbiturates.

Pianist Bobby Henderson, known also as, Robert Bolden Henderson, who accompanied Billie Holiday from 1931-1934, died at age 59, December 9, 1969, in Albany. New York.

Joe Glaser, Billie Holiday's agent, died in 1969 at age 72. Upon his death, ABC, the company Joe Glaser formed with Louis Armstrong was ceded in full to Sidney Korshak, who was an infamous Mob, Labor, and Hollywood lawyer and fixer.

Louis (Satchmo, Pops) Armstrong had a successful jazz entertainment career. He died in NYC in 1971 at age 69. He and his heirs were defrauded of his share in ABC, the booking company Joe Glaser formed with him in the 1930s.

In 1971, Janis Joplin helped purchase a headstone for Bessie Smith. Shamefully, Bessie Smith's estranged husband, Jack Gee, who inherited her estate, left her in an unmarked grave. The pair married in 1923 and separated in 1930. The marker reads, "The Greatest Blues Singer in the World will never stop singing.[103]"

In 1971, Pianist Sonny White, former boyfriend, who accompanied Billie Holiday in 1939, died at age 53 in New York.

In 1972, Assata Shakur was arrested for an armed robbery in the Bronx, New York. Like Billie Holiday, even though Assata was injured and incapable of fleeing, she was handcuffed to her hospital bed and suffered indignities by law enforcement. She escaped prison in 1979 and became a political refuge in Cuba where she has remained for over 40 years.

Duke Ellington reigned in Jazz for over half a century. He died at age 75 in 1974 in New York. He was buried in Woodlawn Cemetery in Bronx, New York.

Linda Lipnack Kuehl, a New York journalist, who preserved recorded interview tapes from associates and friends of Billie Holiday for a biography she never completed, died February 4, 1978, in Washington, DC after attending a Count Basie concert. The death was ruled a suicide. Linda's sister believed her death was foul play.

Charles Mingus Jr., bassist, pianist, composer, an associate and friend of Billie Holiday and Lester Young, died at age 56, in Cuernavaca, Mexico, January 5, 1979.

Count Basie reigned in Jazz for over half a century too. The Count Basie Center for the Arts was named for Count Basie in 1984. The facility, created in 1926, was once the

Reade's Carlton Theater in Red Bank, New Jersey where Count Basie was born. Count Basie is known as the favorite son of Red Bank. He died at age 79 in Hollywood, Florida.

Maely Bartholomew Dufty, mother of Bevan Dufty, wife of William (Bill) Dufty, dear friend of Billie Holiday, who was formerly a publicist, died at age 66 in 1984.

On September 3, 1985, Drummer Jo Jones, Count Basie Orchestra, died at age 73 in New York, New York. He was buried at the Calverton National Cemetery in Calverton, Suffolk County, New York.

John Hammond, who gave Billie Holiday her first record deal, died in 1987, at age 76. He was buried in the prestigious Vanderbilt Family Cemetery and Mausoleum in Staten Island, New York.

Miles Davis, one of the greatest jazz icons in history, died at age 65 in 1991 in Santa Monica, California. He was buried among the jazz greats in Woodlawn Cemetery, Bronx, New York.

Billy Eckstine, a jazz and pop singer died at age 78 in 1993 in Pittsburg, Pennsylvania. He was cremated; his ashes were given to his family and close friends.

Jazz Singer Carmen McRae, a native of Harlem, whose parents were Jamaican immigrants and neighbors of Billie Holiday, said Billie Holiday was her sole musical influencer. Carmen McRae became a great jazz singer. McRae spoke at the Hollywood Walk of Fame ceremony honoring Billie Holiday, April 7, 1986, on Lady Day's 71st heavenly birthday. Carmen recorded *Fine and Mellow,* one of her idol's former tunes in 1988. Carmen died in Hollywood, California, at age 74, on November 10, 1994.

Miles Davis's tombstone reflected his larger-than-life presence in the world of Jazz.

Ella Fitzgerald reigned in jazz for over 60 years. She died in Beverly Hills, California at age 79 in 1996. She was buried at Inglewood Park Cemetery, Inglewood, Los Angeles County, California at the Sunset Mission Mausoleum, Second Floor, Sanctuary of the Bells, Crypt 1063.

Jazz Journalist Leonard Feather spoke at Billie Holiday's Walk of Fame ceremony in 1986 too. He and his wife Jane's only daughter was named Billie Jane Lee Lorraine Feather for her godmother Billie Holiday. Leonard died at age 80 in California.

Billie Jane Lee Lorraine Feather goes by Lorraine Feather today. She is a lyricist, jazz singer and a three-time Grammy nominee and a seven-time Emmy nominee living in Western New York State.

In 1972, Diana Ross sang the soundtrack for *Lady Sings the Blues*. Her tunes in the movie included Billie Holiday tunes *Lady Sings the Blues*, *'Tain't Nobody's Bizness If I Do*, *You've Changed*, *My Man*, *All of Me*, *God Bless the Child*... Diana Ross played Billie Holiday and Billy Dee Williams played Louis McKay. Louis McKay consulted the screenwriters. The film was based on *Lady Sings the Blues*, Billie Holiday's autobiography. Billy Dee portrayed Louis as a sober, levelheaded, protective, business manager of Billie Holiday. Diana Ross and Billy Dee Williams won the NAACP Image Awards for Outstanding Actor/Actress in a Motion Picture.

Louis McKay lived well from his royalties and fees from Billie Holiday's estate. He died at age 72 in 1981 in Camden, Camden County, New Jersey. He was buried at Harleigh Cemetery. At the time of his death, he had a lifetime membership in the NAACP. His will bequeathed his widow Bernice Doris Johnson Yancey McKay 20 percent of his estate and two sons by previous marriages Louis McKay Jr. and Craig obtained the remainder of the estate.

Louis McKay earned an estimated $15,000 to $20,000 each year in royalties from *Lady Sings the Blues*. In 1981, Billie Holiday's estate was worth $1,000,000 and earning $121,212 per year. New Jersey law allowed Bernice to obtain one-third of the augmented estate; her lawyer advised her to take the latter. She did.

In 2012, Bernice sold Billie Holiday's estate to Bicycle Music, an independent publisher. Bicycle Music merged with Concord Music Group in 2015. Billie Holiday's estate was worth $14 million in 2014. Her music continues to sell worldwide[104]. According to the obituary of Bernice Doris McKay, she had other assets. She formerly owned a Furrier, and operated R&B Grocer in New York City.

Louis McKay's widow Bernice Yancey McKay, died in Camden, Camden County, New Jersey, at age 95, October 13, 2021, eight months after *The United States vs. Billie Holiday* staring Audrey Day and directed by Lee Daniels was released on Hulu February 26, 2021. The film was based on the book *Chasing the Scream: The First and Last Days of The War on Drugs* by bestselling author Johann Hari.

During the digital age of music, Columbia Records reissued nine volumes of *The Quintessential Billie Holiday* - 1987. Decca released *The Complete Decca Recordings of Billie Holiday* - 1991, and Verve issued *The Complete Billie Holiday on Verve 1945-1959* - 1993.

Abel Meeropol died in 1986 at the age of 83 in Longmeadow, Massachusetts. Abel Meeropol sustained his family from music publishing fees from *Strange Fruit* and another song, *The House I Live In*, he wrote which was made popular by Frank Sinatra. He and his wife Anne adopted Michael and Robert Rosenberg after their parents Julius and Ethel were executed for espionage by the U.S.A. government.

Pianist Teddy Wilson succumbed to stomach cancer in 1986 at age 73 in New Britain, Connecticut. During the final years of his life, Teddy Wilson performed with two of his sons: Theodore Wilson on bass and Steven Wilson on drums.

Barney Josephson, who owned Café Society and led the way to integrate jazz clubs in New York City died in 1988 at age 86 in New York City; his club boosted the careers of top artist in the 20th century such as Billie Holiday, Hazel Scott, Lena Horne, Sarah Vaughan, Big Joe Turner...

Teddy Wilson's headstone was dedicated by Japanese fans. Photo uploaded by Scott Stanton. Fairview Cemetery, New Britain, Hartford County, Connecticut. U.S.A.

In 1999, *Strange Fruit* was named the song of the century by *Time Magazine*.

In 2000, Billie Holiday was inducted into the Rock and Roll Hall of Fame. Diana Ross presented the award.

Billie Holiday: Jazz Singer

In 2002, The Library of Congress listed *Strange Fruit* in the National Sound Registry.

Lionel Hampton, a drummer, pianist, and singer, died at age 94 in 2002 in New York. He raised funds and constructed the Lionel Hampton Houses in the 1960s and two other projects afterward. He was buried at Woodlawn Cemetery in Bronx, New York.

In 2005, a saxophone, played by legendary Charlie Parker was auctioned for $250,000.00. Yet he died unable to perform and earn a living from his talent – artistically banned as an entertainer by the Cabaret license program.

Artie Shaw, known as the King of the Clarinet in the 1930s, was afterward off and on with music. He died at age 94 in 2004. In 1938, his band produced the hits, *Yesterdays*, *Out of Nowhere*, *Nightmare*, *Nightmare*, *Softly As in a Morning Sunrise*, and *Any Old Time* with Billie Holiday. He later became a novelist. He performed in London, England in 1992.

Max Roach, drummer/composer, whose quartet played background in 1947 for *I'm A Fool To Want You* by Billie Holiday, died at age 83, in 2007. He played drums on other tunes. He was laid to rest at Woodlawn Cemetery near other jazz greats.

Billie Holiday's godson, Bevan Dufty, son of William and Maely Dufty was elected and served multiple terms (2002 – 2011) on the San Francisco Board of Supervisors.

On November 27, 2017, NYC Mayor De Blasio signed legislation repealing the 91-year-old Cabaret Law established in 1926 during prohibition which prohibited Billie Holiday and her peers from performing and entertaining participants of NYC's nightlight after their drug and other convictions. The Cabaret Licensing program economically crippled NYC artists, especially Black artists.

Sylvia Syms, an English actress, who was interviewed in the 1970s by Linda Lipnack Kuehl about her friendship with Billie Holiday died Jan. 27, 2023, at age 89 at Danville Hall, a retirement home for actors and actresses in London, England.[105]

Lester (Prez) Young's son Dr. Lester Young Jr., born in 1947, became the first Black Chancellor of the Board of Regents in January 2021. The office was established in 1784. The New York legislature appointed Dr. Young to serve as a Regent at Large in 2008. He has been a public servant in New York for over 50 years.

Lester Young's daughter, Yvette (Beverly) Young, born in

1957, is also an educator.

Sylvia Syms, New York, N.Y., June 1947 William P. Gottlieb.

The annual Lester Young & Charlie Parker Birthday Festival, a three-day festival, highlighting both saxophonists started August 27-28, 2022, at Columbia University in New York, New York. Prez's birthday is August 27th and Bird's birthday is on the 29th.

Fans can visit The Billie Holiday Experience on YouTube which gives them access to 122 videos. The page has 17K subscribers. Billie Holiday has a social media presence on Facebook, Instagram, and Twitter. The legacy of Lady Day lives on through her music, films, stories, and video footage.

Seven

Legacy

"No innovator was like her. Nobody![106]" Drummer Jo Jones, a friend who accompanied Billie Holiday during the Swing and Bebop era, said emphatically.

Billie Holiday lives through her music. During her 30-year singing career, she released 38 charting singles and sang over 350 different tunes. Though Billie Holiday never learned how to read music and her voice was limited in range, she phrased words beautifully and her voice was the defining voice in jazz for her generation.

She influenced 20th and 21st century artists including the Great Frank Sinatra and others such as Etta James, Janis Joplin, Joni Mitchell, Tony Bennett, Bob Dylan, Sam Cooke, Marvin Gaye, Sting, Bono, Cassandra Wilson, Amy Winehouse, Tawanna Shaunte, and Adele. Today, Billie Holiday's music sells more than any of her jazz female contemporaries.

American trumpeter, composer, and teacher Wynton Marsalis, a native of New Orleans, Louisiana, who was born October 18, 1961, recalled listening to Billie Holiday records, rather than Louis Armstrong, Dizzy Gillespie, or other musicians who were expert trumpeters, every day for one year in the mid-1980s. Jazz greats noted, Billie Holiday used her voice as an instrument. Listening to Billie

Billie Holiday: Jazz Singer

Holiday music gave Wynton Marsalis lessons on rhythm, phrasing, and sophistication suitable as great training for a jazz student.

Billie Holiday, backstage, Carnegie Hall, 1948, by William P. Gottlieb, Library of Congress.

Billie Holiday was one of the highest paid performers in her era; but her earnings were wasted on her vices and mismanaged by her two husbands and two other key male lover/managers. She was a singer and song writer, who recomposed simple songs into hits. She co-wrote *Don't Explain*, *Fine and Mellow*, *God Bless the Child*, and *Lady Sings the Blues.* Two of Lady Day's best jazz recordings,

This Year's Kisses and *Mean to Me* were produced with Prez, Lester Young. Billie and Lester were hipsters and trendsetters in the jazz genre. For 12 years, from 1947 to 1959, Billie was forced to earn a living without the legal ability to work in NYC jazz clubs.

Billie Holiday's generation pushed away from the showbiz norms of Black entertainers who displayed bulging eyes - happy character norms established during the Vaudeville variety show entertainment era (1880 – 1930). Lady Day, Prez, Sweets, Bird, Miles, and others incorporated individualism into their entertainment styles. Prez wore pork pie hats, black over coats, and sunglasses on stage inside facilities and outdoors; he dusted insults off his shoulders with a mini broom, while she wore her signature gardenias, elegant gowns, and furs. Jazz wheeled in a 'cool,' authentic, and relaxed flow which remains present in entertainment. Miles Davis was the king of 'cool.' He wore his Blackness with honor.

Pianist Ahmad Jamal, 92, one of the last surviving and active jazz greats from the Swing era praised the jazz icons who preceded him. "I don't distinguish Bach or Beethoven from Duke Ellington," he declared. "Without Louis Armstrong, Billy Strayhorn, Sidney Bechet, or Don Byas, the Beatles wouldn't have existed, not anything that came after them," he added. "Music no longer exists. "You turn on the TV and you never see Billie Holiday...[107]," he concluded.

Ahmad Jamal was formerly known as Frederick Russell Jones. John Hammond signed Ahmad Jamal and The Three Strings to Okeh Records in 1951 after seeing the band play at the Embers in New York City. The Three Strings which played at Chicago's Blue Note in the early

Billie Holiday: Jazz Singer

1950s was renamed The Ahmad Jamal Trio. Great jazz legends including Billie Holiday performed at Chicago's Blue Note. Ahmad Jamal passed April 16, 2023, weeks before his 93rd birthday.

Sonny Rollins, age 93, is one of the last surviving jazz greats. He recorded with Coleman Hawkins, his idol, and played in venues with Lester Young, Charlie Parker, Dizzy Gillespie, Max Roach, Miles Davis, Ben Webster, Lena Horne, Ella Fitzgerald, Billie Holiday, and others.

Sonny declared, "Jazz transcends life and death as we know it on this planet."

"Jazz is more universal – eternal[108]," he added.

Time magazine wrote two sentences as a summation of the life and times of the Great Jazz Singer Billie Holiday known as Lady Day which are as follows:

> Died. Billie Holiday, Negro blues singer, whose husky, melancholy voice reflected the tragedy of her own life, in Manhattan. Born of indigent teenagers, schooled in a Baltimore brothel, she stubbornly nursed her resentment, poured it out in songs that reached their height of popularity in the early '40s – *Billie Blues*, *The Man I Love*, above all, *Strange Fruit*, a description of a Negro lynching in the South – succumbed to the dope addiction which dogged her to the end[109].

The poem *Strange Fruit* written by Abel Meerepol was a description of a chilling photograph of the 1930 public lynching of Thomas Shipp and Abram Smith in Marion, Indiana which was in the north rather than in the south.

189

Not everyone felt Billie Holiday's voice was related to tragedies in her life. Wynton Marsalis, Artistic Director of Jazz at the Lincoln Center, argued the quality of Lady Day's voice was not connected to the hardships she faced in her life. She simply had 'it.' Her having 'it' is why she became known as one of the greatest voices in the history of jazz. Wynton Marsalis's other jazz idol was Miles Davis.

Wynton Marsalis plays classical and jazz music. He played at the Symphony Center, in Chicago in January of 2023. His concert Gallery tickets started at $133 per seat. Balcony seats were $324. Seats are much higher than they were when Billie Holiday first sang at Carnegie Hall in 1947. The starting price for her concert tickets was $2.25. Jazz has survived. Billie Holiday's music survived. Today, she is known in all corners of the world for her distinct lyrical phrasing and personable singing.

Billie Holiday is praised as a singer who bent notes like a horn player in the band. James Lincoln Collier said of her music from 1935-45, "More than nearly any other singer, Holiday phrased her performances in the manner of a jazz instrumental soloist and accordingly she has to be seen as a complete jazz musician, not just a singer[110]."

Billie Holiday is known for having song lyrics from the inside rather than the outside. Frank Sinatra sang from the inside too. Ross Porter, CEO, Toronto Jazz Radio station, said, "She delivered recorded performances so commanding they can still bring one to tears. It is the sound of a woman who sings from the centre of the song.[111]"

She restructured singing as an art form with breathtaking phrasing such as the way she presented the last word "crop" in the last line of *Strange Fruit* at the end "Here is a strange and bitter crop." Her performance said to white listeners your society's mob justice of unlawfully destroying Black bodies is evil and wrong.

Bandleader and Jazz/Pop Singer Billy Eckstine declared, "She was not a show woman. If she gave the impression, she didn't give a shit what her audience thought, it was because she was singing not for them but for eternity.

William Dufty agreed proposing, "Billy Holiday knew in her bones that a thousand years from now, as long as the language endures, people will still listen to her singing and be moved by it. Call it arrogance, serenity, hallucination, there it was[112]."

"To the people in our industry, she was the greatest lady of all time. She was the queen bee. Without even trying she was one of the most sensual of all the lady singers. I saw the world in that face. All of the beauty and all of the misery. Billy Holiday sang only truth. She knew nothing else," Syvia Syms, fellow singer and friend of Billie Holiday, said January 20th, 1973, in an interview with Linda Lipnack Huehl[113].

In 1972, 13 years after the death of Billie Holiday a theater was established in her honor in Bedford-Stuyvesant, in Brooklyn, NY, the second largest Black neighborhood in the U.S.A. The Billie Holiday Theater with a 218-seating capacity is a hub for the arts and local talents. Well-known actors, writers, designers, and musicians obtained their start in the theater including Samuel L. Jackson, Debbie Allen, Bill Cobbs, Phyllis Yvonne Stickney, Carol Woods, Elaine Graham, Ebony JoAnn ...

Noted individuals in the arts such as Lena Horne, Max Roach, Eubie Blake, Stephanie Mills, Ben Vereen, Jay-Z, Franklin Augustus Thomas, Nas, Biggie Smalls, and others are from Bedford-Stuyvesant and Brooklyn. The Billie Holiday Theater has been a jewel for Black art for over 50 years. Franklin A. Thomas used his position as the first Black president of the Ford Foundation to invest in his community; he secured money for the Bedford-Stuyvesant Restoration Corporation and the Restoration Plaza. The Billie Holiday Theater is located at 1368 Fulton Street in the Restoration Plaza in Brooklyn, New York. Lady Day's last residence in Unit B, an Upper West Side brownstone, constructed in 1910, was listed for $13,995 million dollars in September of 2022[114].

Billie Holiday and Frank Sinatra, both born in 1915, both loved worldwide, are two of the greatest intimate singers of all time. In 1985, Baltimore, Maryland Sculptor James Earl Reid created an 8 feet 6 inches tall bronze statue of Billie Holiday depicting the artist in a strapless gown with gardenias in her hair and her mouth open. Mayor William Donald Schaefer dedicated the $113,000 statute. Restoration of the statute in 2008 cost $76,000.

Billie Holiday: Jazz Singer

Over the years, Billie Holiday has been honored in song and in theater. In 1986, the play *Lady Day at Emerson's Bar and Grill* debuted in New York. The play is an intimate event that allows audiences the opportunity to meet Billie Holiday's character in March of 1959 - the month Lester Young died and four months before Billie's death July 17, 1959. Actors sing Billie Holiday classics such as *What A Little Moonlight Can Do*, *Gimme A Pigfoot and Bottle of Beer*, *God Bless the Child*, *Crazy He Calls Me*, *Strange Fruit*, and *Tain't Nobody's Biz-ness If I Do*.

Lady Day at Emerson's Bar and Grill ran in Buffalo, New York in the 1990s. The play featuring George Caldwell and Alex McArthur at the MusicalFare Theater's Premier Cabaret ran January 18 – January 29, 2023, at Daemen University in Amherst, New York. Students and groups obtained discounted tickets for $40.00. The event entertained the audience with comical and factual tales about Billie Holiday's two husbands, male managers, her mother, the legal system, racism, and her career.

In March of 1989, Playwright Lanie Robertson's Cabaret Tribute in the form of a one woman play presented *Lady Day at Emerson's Bar and Grill*. The role of Billie Holiday was played by Gail Nelson, who song 15 popular tunes of Billie Holiday including *What a Little Moon Light Can Do*, *God Bless the Child*, *I Wonder Where Our Love Has Gone?*...

April 10, 2015, 100 years and three days after Billie's birth, Cassandra Wilson, a native of Jackson, Mississippi and one of the most successful modern jazz singers, honored Billie Holiday in song at the Apollo Theater which was the first stage Billie Holiday performed on when the theater first opened in 1934. Billie Holiday made a splash on

American music with her bluesy jazz singing. Her unique renditions, phrasing, pitch, and timing continues to move listeners worldwide over 64 years after her death.

The voice of Lady Day continues to warm hearts and influence singers and instrumentalists. Billie Holiday was one of the first commercially successful recorded Black protest singers in the U.S.A. She advocated that Black people should have the right to listen to her sing at jazz clubs in Los Angeles, California and influenced jazz club owners to lift their segregation policies before the Civil Rights movement took root. According to Rev. Nicole Duncan-Smith, Lady Day broke social norms... *Strange Fruit* was not just a cute, little ditty, but her "I HAVE a Dream" offering to the world[115].

Billie Holiday was a race woman, who risked her life for the betterment of her race. She was also a pioneer, and one of the greatest jazz vocalists. Lady Day used *Strange Fruit* as a political tool to advance the civil rights of Black people living in American. Like Frank Sinatra, Lady Day remains universally known around the globe. As William "Bill" Dufty once said, "Holiday doesn't sing songs; she transforms them.[116]" As Nat Hentoff proclaimed, "Billie, by the time she was in her twenties, had created a way of singing that was unmistakably her own[117]."

Lorraine Feather, Goddaughter of Billie Holiday, noted on Lady Day's legacy:

> There are always scores of talented performers in music, but the era that my father covered during his lifetime was a golden age in jazz, in that there were musicians and vocalists in the forefront who not only possessed stunning instruments and musicality but sounded like no

Billie Holiday: Jazz Singer

one else. Billie Holiday has had many imitators, but her voice and style were inimitable, and the terrible sadness of her time on Earth flowed through every note she sang.

To me, the most memorable Billie Holiday song is *Strange Fruit* because it is unique. The lyrics are about a period in American history that is so horrific and shameful, it's almost unbelievable that it was written and sung. I was told that after BH performed it she could not and would not sing anything else on any given night. I also loved the early Billie Holiday songs that were light-hearted, like *Your Mother's Son-in-Law* and *Them There Eyes*[118].

New Bourbon Street Jazz Band of Jackson, Mississippi Banjo player Ron Welch, dubbed *Strange Fruit* his favorite Billie Holiday song also. "She sang it to people who needed to hear it. She was a prophet before James Meredith (Mississippi Second Reconstruction icon). She reminded us, where we went wrong[119]."

Billie Holiday sang *Strange Fruit* for the first time in 1938. She recorded *Strange Fruit* in 1939. It became her bestselling record. In 1978, The National Endowment for the Arts listed *Strange Fruit* on its 'Songs of the Century' list. *Strange Fruit* was also inducted into the Grammy Hall of Fame[120].

Jazz enthusiast Schuyler Manning recalled, after nibbling on a platter of Tamale Nachos, during Jazz with Raphael Semmes Quartet intermission at Hal & Mals restaurant in Jackson, Mississippi, being introduced to the music of Billie Holiday in 1981 in his 9th grade High School Vocal Jazz Class in St. Louis, Missouri. "My favorite Billie Holiday song is *Lady Sings the Blues*[121]."

Jazz icons Lester Bowie, Charles Creath, Miles Davis, Wynton Marsalis, and Al Jarreau hail from St. Louis. Make no mistake about it, it would please all the jazz gods, if public education offered jazz appreciation courses around the globe. Acquiring Jazz history will inspire millions to pursue various career paths in the music industry such as: booking agents, producers, record label owners, vocalists, instrumentalists, song writers, band leaders, public relation administrators, record keepers, etc.

Knowledge of the Black American musical experience in this country will awaken our youth to personal truths. The stories of perseverance and greatness are priceless. Imagine the impact of youth learning how average people became great repeatedly. Imagine the possibilities of learning how artists from humble beginnings who look like you became icons.

The 1972 film *Lady Sings the Blues* featuring Diana Ross and Billy D. Williams which played throughout the 1980s introduced a generation to key Billy Holiday songs including *Lady Sings the Blues*.

> Lady Sings the Blues lyrics.
>
> Lady sings the blues
> She's got them bad
> She feels so sad
> And wants the world to know
> Just what her blues is all about
>
> Lady sings the blues
> She tells her side
> Nothing to hide
> Now the world will know

Billie Holiday: Jazz Singer

> Just what her blues is all about
>
> Songwriters: Billie Holiday, Herbie Nichols[122]

Whether or not Billie Holiday had the blues bad as the lyrics in *Lady Sings the Blues* described, she had a voice which ushered in a new sound in 1933; her delivery of *Strange Fruit* in 1939 reshaped music by exposing discrimination in song, and she influenced jazz and pop vocalists as well as instrumentalists in various genres. Henry Pleasants, a music critic, discovered and fell in love with Billie Holiday's voice in 1959, after her passing. He noted, like John Hammond and Miles Davis, that Billie Holiday used her voice as an instrument.

The article excerpt is as follows:

> That Billie Holiday was blessed with an extraordinary instrument isn't immediately apparent even to those who admire her. As Henry Pleasants put it, she had "a meager voice–small, hoarse at the bottom and thinly shrill on top, with top and bottom never very far apart[123]."

Drea Dominique released *I'll Be Seeing You*, an old Billie Holiday classic, in January of 2023, after the Pandemic which produced unprecedented loss of loved ones. Drea has a smooth R&B and Hip-Hop voice. Frank Sinatra recorded his version of *I'll Be Seeing You* in 1962. Rod Stewart, Norah Jones, Tony Bennett, Willie Nelson, and others have also recorded the old tune.

"Even one person giving up hope is too many but thankfully, music often serves as a remedy to a wounded soul[124]," Drea Dominique proposed.

Jackson, Mississippi Jazz lover Shirley Shaw Bracey dubbed smiling, "*God Bless the Child*[125]" her favorite Billie Holiday song. Mrs. Bracey, WJSU Development Assistant Membership, gave her comment while serving in her official capacity for Jackson State University's WJSU Jazz radio station @ 88.5 FM dial conducting a membership and donation drive to a jazz crowd at Hal & Mals restaurant.

Two generations after the end of American slavery, jazz musicians channeled their rage against a nation's constant injustices into a contemporary music form – Jazz. Today, Jazz reaches out and touches the universe daily. Jazz warms soul and hearts from Miami to Maine, from Canada to the Congo, and from Algeria to Athens. The swing genre of jazz started in New Orleans before the birth of Billie Holiday. Jazz emerged from blues, the Dixieland sound, and Ragtime and shifted to swing to bebop and from bebop to cool and from cool (free jazz) to fusion.

Billie Holiday improvised like people she admired: Prez and Louis. She changed tunes and made the songs her own. She phrased, like no one else, with supple inventiveness and graceful wit. When Billie Holiday sang *Fine and Mellow* on the Sound of Jazz in 1957, her performance was so powerful the musicians cried in the control room.

Billie Holiday is an international icon known worldwide as Lady Day. Artifacts of Billie Holiday are preserved at the National Museum of African American History & Culture at the Smithsonian located at 1400 Constitution Avenue Northwest in Washington, District of Columbia 20560 where she is classified as an American jazz singer, songwriter, actress and an icon in American culture.

On display are famous photographs of Billie Holiday with her last husband Louis McKay, and other celebrities including Louis Armstrong; several of her master discs: *My Man*, *Lover Come Back to Me*, *Stormy Weather*, and *Yesterdays* are preserved. Her exhibit also includes a photograph of Billie Holiday and her dog Mister; a cocktail dress worn by Billie Holiday; a *Lady Sings the Blues* film poster; and a gown and a costume hat worn by Diana Ross in the film and other memorabilia.

On April 30, 2023, Jazz Great Herbie Hancock, who emerged in the industry during the Bebop era and is a jazz rock icon, hosted the 12th Annual International Jazz Day which celebrated the rich history of jazz and this music genre's international impact. Performances hailed from Beijing, Beirut, Casablanca, Fairbanks, Honolulu, Johannesburg, Marondera, New York, Paris, Rio De Janiero, San Francisco, Vienna, and Washington, DC. Herbie Hancock said wearing a black shirt, seated on a piano stool in front of a black piano, "We invite you… honoring the spirit of creativity, collaboration, and community that jazz personifies. International Jazz Day unites the world.[126]"

Yesterday, a jazz trio, a jazz quartet, or a house band played *Bye Bye Black Bird,* a jazz standard; *Somewhere Over the Rainbow,* a Duke Ellington's composition; *General Pilot,* a Herbie Hancock track; *Mr. Magic*, a Grover Washington piece; and *God Bless the Child*, a classic co-written by Billie Holiday, to a dinner crowd, at a school concert, or at a festival.

Tomorrow, a jazz trio, a jazz quartet, or a school band will play *Sentimental Mood* - Duke Ellington; *Mercy, Mercy, Mercy* – Cannonball Adderley; *Take the A Train* - Duke Ellington, *My Funny Valentine* - Miles Davis, *Unforgettable* – Nat King Cole, and *All or Nothing At All* – Billie Holiday.

Today, Jazz is available on CDs, on vinyl, or it can be streamed. Jazz is here to stay forevermore!

Billie Holiday is the great lady of song; she is etched in history with King Oliver, Louis Armstrong, Duke Ellington, Fletcher Henderson, Count Basie, Coleman Hawkins, Lester Young, Jo Jones, Ben Webster, Charlie Parker, Charles Mingus, Miles Davis, Ella Fitzgerald, Sarah Vaughan, Nancy Wilson, Dizzy Gillespie, John Coltrane, Wayne Shorter, Sonny Rollins....

Billie Holiday's classic songs dwell in the hearts and souls of music lovers 64 years and counting after her passing. Jazz is a gift to the world! It was developed out of the bowels of the American Black experience from the rat, tat dancing and beats from West Africa to the roots of blues in Clarksdale, Mississippi. And the beat goes on. Thank you. More, more, more!

Partial List of Protest Songs:

1. *Oh, Freedom, post-Civil War Negro Spiritual,* 1850
2. *Lift Every Voice and Sing,* James Weldon Johnson 1905
3. *Alabama Song,* Kurt Weill 1925
4. *Strange Fruit,* Billie Holiday 1939
5. *This Land is Your Land*, Woody Guthrie, 1940
6. *Sixteen Tons,* Merle Travis 1946
7. *We Shall Overcome*, Pete Seeger 1948
8. *Chain Gang,* Sam Cooke 1960

Billie Holiday: Jazz Singer

9. *The Times They Are A-Changing*, Bob Dylan, 1964
10. *Mississippi Goddam*, Nina Simone 1964
11. *A Change is Gonna Come*, Sam Cooke 1965
12. *Strange Fruit*, Nina Simone 1965
13. *Say it Loud: I'm Black and I'm Proud*, James Brown 1968
14. *Freedom* Suite 1969
15. *The Revolution Will Not Be Televised*, Gil Scott Heron 1970
16. *What's Going On*, Marvin Gaye 1971
17. *Imagine*, John Lennon 1971
18. *I'll Take You There*, The Staple Singers 1972
19. *Get Up, Stand Up*, Bob Marley 1973
20. *Born in the U.S.A.*, Bruce Springsteen 1984
21. *Fuck the Police*, NWA 1988
22. *Fight the Power*, Public Enemy, 1989
23. *Killing in the Name*, Rage Against the Machine 1992
24. *Revolution* Arrested Development 1992
25. *To Pimp a Butterfly*, Kendrick Lamar 2015
26. *Alright*, Kendrick Lamar 2015
27. *The Bigger Picture* Lil Baby 2020
28. *Riots: How Many Times* Trey Songz 2020
29. *Rockstar* by DaBaby ft Roddy Ricch 2020

Grammy Award (posthumously):

Grammy Lifetime Achievement Award 1987
Best Historical Album for recordings:
   1. Lady Day: The Complete Billie Holiday
   2. The Complete Billie Holiday
   3. Billie Holiday – The Complete Decca Recording
   4. Billie Holiday – Giants of Jazz

Billie Holiday songs/albums inducted into the **Grammy Hall of Fame:**

1. *My Man* 1937
2. *Embraceable You* 1944
3. *Crazy He Calls Me* 1945
4. *Lover Man* 1945
5. *God Bless the Child* 1976
6. *Strange Fruit* 1978
7. Best Historical Album Grammy 1979
8. *Giants of Jazz*, 1980
9. *Billie Holiday: The Complete Decca Recordings* 1992
10. *The Complete Billie Holiday* 1994
11. *Lover Man 1989*
12. *Lady in Satin* 2000
13. *Lady Day: The Complete Billie Holiday* 2002
14. *Embraceable You* 2005
15. *Crazy He Calls Me*, 2010

VH1 ranked Billie Holiday # 6 on its 100 Greatest Women in Rock n' Roll list in 1999.

Musical Inductions:
1. Grammy Hall of Fame 1973
2. Rock and Roll Hall of Fame 2000
3. Nesuhis Ertegun Jazz Hall of Fame 2004
4. National Women's Hall of Fame 2011
5. The Apollo Theater Walk of Fame 2015
6. Philadelphia Music Alliance Walk of Fame 2015
7. National Rhythm & Blues Hall of Fame 2017

Famous Albums:
1. *The Lady Sings* 1956
2. *Velvet Mood* 1956
3. *Body and Soul* 1957
4. *Stay with Me* 1958
5. *All or Nothing at All* 1958
6. *Lady in Satin* 1958

Billie Holiday received a **Hollywood Walk of Fame Star** on April 7, 1976, which was her 71st heavenly birthday.

On September 18, 1994, the U.S. Postal Service issued a stamp in her honor in the *Jazz & Blues Singers* series.

The Irish rock group U2 released a Billie Holiday tribute song titled *Angel of Harlem* in 1988.

Broadway Productions on Billie Holiday:
Yesterdays: An Evening With Billie Holiday, 2011, featuring Vanessa Rubin

Lady Day at Emerson's Bar & Grill, 2014, featuring Audry McDonald. She was awarded the Tony Award for Best Performance by an Actress in a Leading Role in a Play for the portrayal of Billie Holiday.

Lady Day at Emerson's Bar & Grill, Sept. 14 through Oct. 8, 2023, Baltimore Center Stage, 700 N. Calvert Street, Baltimore, MD 21202.

Books about Billie Holiday and Jazz Greats:
1. *Lady Sings the Blues* by Billie Holiday with William Dufty 1956, 2006
2. *Lady Day: The Many Faces of Billie Holiday* by Robert O'Meally 1991
3. *If You Can't Be Free: Be a Mystery* by Farah Jasmine Griffin 2001
4. *Strange Fruit: Billie Holiday and the Biography of a Song* by David Margolick 2001
5. *Billie Holiday: Wishing on the Moon* by Donald Clarke 2002
6. *Billie Holiday: A Biography* by Meg Greene 2006

7. *With Billie: A New Look at the Unforgettable Lady Day* by Julia Blackburn 2006
8. *Billie Holiday: The Musician and the Myth* by John Szwed 2015
9. *Chasing the Scream: The First and Last Days of the War on Drugs* by Johann Hari 2015
10. *Willow, Weep For Me: The Life of Billie Holiday* by Nigel Barnes 2019
11. *Billie Holiday: Jazz Singer* by Meredith Coleman McGee 2024

Billie Holiday's 1956 autobiography *Lady Sings the Blues* was made into a firm *Lady Sings the Blue* in 1972 starring Diana Ross and Billy Dee Williams.

March 5, 2020. *Time* magazine listed 1939: Billie Holiday - 100 Women of the Year.

February 26, 2021, Andra Day portrayed Billie Holiday in the biopic *The United States v. Billie Holiday*. The film was Directed by Lee Daniels. Andra Day won a Golden Globe for her performance.

March 21, 2021, The Billie Holiday Theatre was awarded the National Medal of Arts by Pres. Joe Biden. Theatre President and CEO Blondel A. Pinnock accepted the medal on behalf of Billie Holiday.

On January 1, 2023, *Rolling Stone* magazine listed Billie Holiday as #4 on its 200 Greatest Singers of All Time list.

On April 13, 2023, Baltimore Museum of Arts displayed Billie Holiday's studio baby picture, taped interviews, and handwritten notes. Billie Holiday is one of the city's poster children representing Black History and Culture.

Billie Holiday: Jazz Singer

Billie Holiday sold over 259,600 albums. Her best-selling album was *The Legend of Billie Holiday* (1985) which sold 100,000 LPs. It went gold. She sold 70,000 LPs of *Lady in Satin* (1958) in the USSR, her second ranking album. *The Essential Billie Holiday* (1993) album sales totaled: 60,000. It went Silver in the UK. *Strange Fruit* (1990) was her 4th bestselling album. It sold 29,600 LPs in the USSR.[127]

In the words of the original and rarest jazz singer to grace the world on how she defines distinctive art, "No two people on earth are alike, and it's got to be that way in music, or it isn't music[128]," Billie Holiday said.

Lester Young and Billie Holiday
Courtesy of the New York Public Library.

Meredith Coleman McGee

St. Raymond's New Cemetery and Mausoleum, Bronx, NY Range 56, Grave 29. Photo by Mario Hemken 10.27.2018.

Lady Day's songs touch the souls and hearts of listeners. Fans place flowers at the graveside of Lady Day & Duchess.

Louis Armstrong mural in downtown Lexington, Kentucky by Carol M. Highsmith. Library of Congress

Billie Holiday: Jazz Singer

Performing Arts mural by Randy Spicer featuring jazz immortal Louis Armstrong, Eureka, California photo by Carol M. Highsmith 2012, Library of Congress

Duke Ellington mural DC, Library of Congress

Billie Holiday, Downbeat, New York, N.Y. Feb. 1947, by William P. Gottlieb, Library of Congress

Charlie Parker (Bird) 1947, Library of Congress

Billie Holiday: Jazz Singer

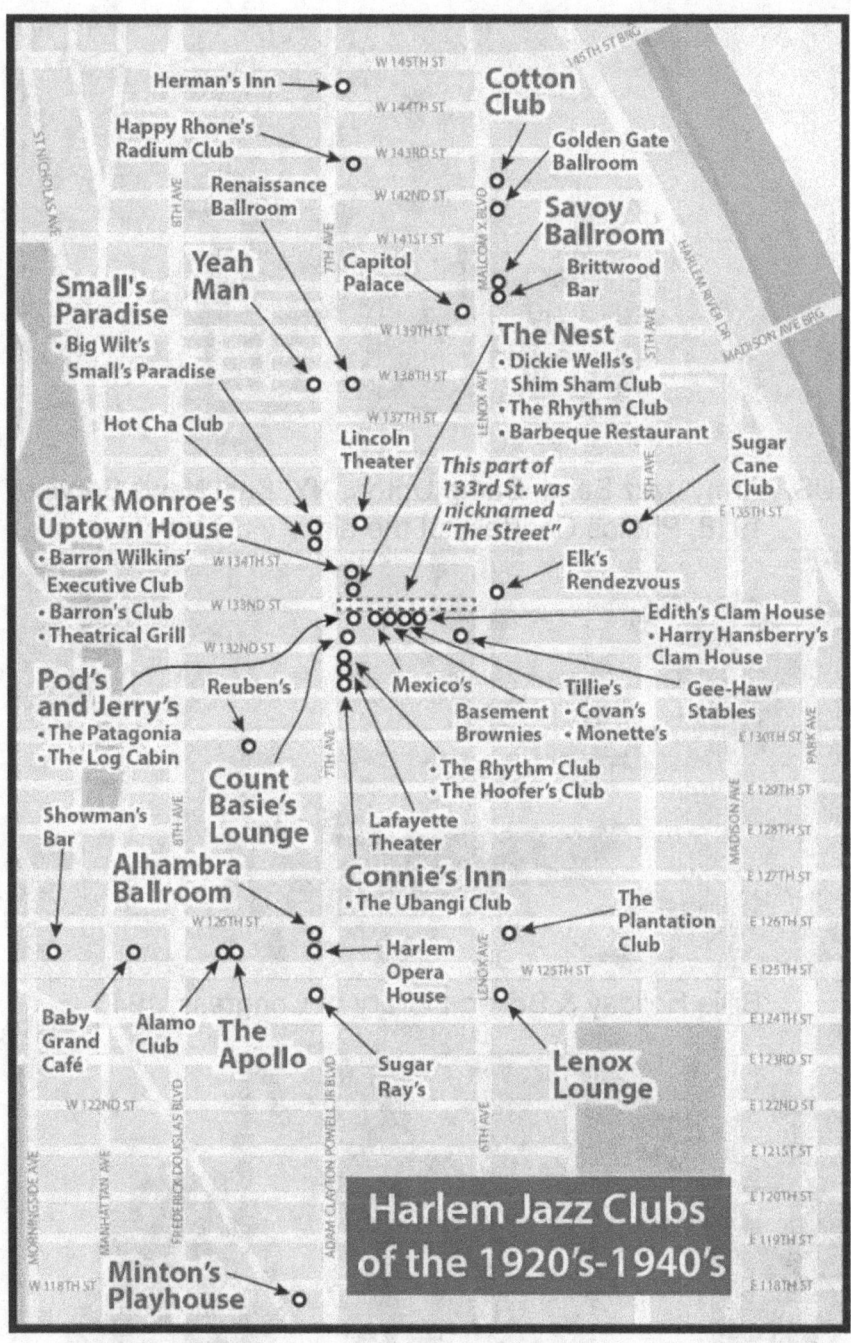

USA Army Jazz Band, Camp Upton, NY, Bain News Service 1918, Photos Courtesy of the Library of Congress

Billie Holiday & Boxer, Library of Congress, 1946

Cicely Tyson and Miles Davis, by Bernard Gotfryd, 1982

ABOUT THE AUTHOR

Meredith Coleman McGee, a poet, a professional writer, book publisher, book collector, lecturer, and small business owner, is the author of six full-length and seven children's books which include: *Billie Holiday: Jazz Singer, Baby Bubba and Kay*, *Juneteenth: Freedom Day, Midnight Moon, Every Inch Love Will, Odyssey, Nashida: Visits Mississippi's Old Capitol Museum*, *James Meredith: Warrior and the America that created him*, *Nashida: Visits the Smith Robertson Museum*, *Nashida: Visits the Mississippi State Capitol*, *Married to Sin* (*Casada al Pecado*), *My Picture Dictionary*, and *My First Book Series*. McGee chairs Community Library Mississippi and promotes early literacy. McGee is a native of Los Angeles, California. She was raised in the Capital City of Jackson, Mississippi.

Meredith Coleman McGee, Author/ Acquisition Editor/ Publisher | Meredith Etc

Email comments to: meredithcmcgee@gmail.com

Follow the author online:
Instagram: meredithetcdotcom
Facebook: meredith.mcgee.31
X (Twitter): meredithetc -- Facebook: meredithetc

Index

Adderley, Cannonball, 173, 200
Ahmad Jamal Trio, 132, 189
All The Things You Are, 72
Allen, Henry (Red), 151
Allied powers, 63
American Record Corporation, 60
Ammons, Albert, 65, 77
Angel of Harlem, 203
Another Woman's Man, 34
Apollo Theater, 13, 37, 65, 69, 129, 159, 193, 202
Armstrong, Louis, 9, 11-15, 17, 19, 26, 32, 34, 40, 45, 47-49, 50, 69, 102-103, 111, 114-115, 122, 135, 151
Aguilera, Christina, 79

Bankhead, Tallulah, 91, 93, 135, 141
Barracoon: The Story of the Last 'Black Cargo,' vii
Barnes, Mae, 135
Basement Brownies, 29
Bechet, Sidney, 151, 188
Belafonte, Harry, 98, 174
Benny Goodman Band, 14
Beyoncé, 59
Berigan, Bunny, 60
The Bernard Peiffer Trio, 152
Bigard, Barney, 45
Biggie Smalls, 192
Big John's Café, 33, 59
Big Joe Turner, 57, 65, 77, 90, 182
Bill's Place, 57
Billie Dove, 15-16, 31
Black Swan Records, 45, 47
Blake, Eubie, 192
Bless My Bones, 167
Blues songs:

Billie Holiday: Jazz Singer

Crazy Blues, 47, *Downhearted Blues,* 47, *I Found My Thrill on Blueberry Hill,* 130, *I Got a Head Like a Rock and a Heart Like a Marble Stone,* 106, *I'm Wild About That Thing,* 11, *Lost Your Head Blues,* 11, *Me and My Gin,* 11, *Rhythm for Sale,* 34, *Sugar Foot Stomp,* 11, *Sweet Georgia Brown,* 11, *Two Old Maids in a Folding Chair,* 34; *Wild Man Blues,* 11, *Willie the Weeper,* 11.

Bowie, Lester, 196
Braff, Ruby, 152
Bracey, Shirley Shaw, 198
Bronzeville, 14
Bryant, Maria, 103, 120

Cabaret license, 15, 118-119, 124, 134-135, 138, 140, 173, 183
Cadillac Records, 21
Caldwell, George, 193
Calloway, Blanche, 9
Calloway, Cab, 3, 9, 14, 101, 122
Calverton National Cemetery, 178
Cardinal Records, 47
Carnegie, Andrew, 14
Carnegie Hall, 14, 67, 122, 132-133, 145-147, 150, 173, 187, 190
Carney, Harry, 45
Carter, Bennie, 33, 156
CBS, 143, 148, 152, 155
Cecil Taylor Quartet, 152
The Chico Hamilton Quintet, 122
Christian, Charlie, 77
Chitlin' Circuit, 8, 14-15
Clayton, Buck, 37, 40, 54, 64, 67, 74, 86, 122, 155, 163
Cohn, Al, 122
Cole, Nat King, 79, 91, 119, 200
Colony Record Shop, 14
Columbia Records, 1, 43, 47, 58, 60, 86-87, 102, 105, 181
Cooke, Sam, 95, 186, 200

213

Coolio, 22
Customhouse Street, 50
Conti Street, 50
Costello, Frank, 33
Costa, Eddie, 152
Connor, Chris, 152
The Cotton Club, 26-28, 30, 58, 94
The Count Basie Center for the Arts, 12, 177
Count Basie and His Orchestra, 138, 152,
Crack Cocaine epidemic, 14
Creath, Charles, 196
Cross, James 'Stump,' 92

Dance Along with Basie, 174
Daniels, Lee, 20, 181, 204
Dave Brubeck Quartet, 152, 173
Davis, Miles, 18, 48-49, 51, 53, 73, 98, 119, 129, 135, 157, 164, 173-174, 178-179, 188-190, 196-197, 200
Davis Jr., Sammy, 98
Day, Andra, 18, 204
Dean, Alice, 13-14, 16
Decca Records, 34, 106, 134, 181, 201
DeFranco, Buddy, 159
Detroit Red, 58, 168
Dickerson, Vic, 106, 153
Dickie Well's Clam House, 58
Dion, Céline, 59
Dizzy Gillespie and His Orchestra, 153
DMX, 21
Dominique, Drea, 197
Domino, Fats, 129-130
Don Eliott Quartet, 152
Douglass, Frederick, ix, xiv
DownBeat, 68, 70, 113-114, 147
Dufty, William, 137, 141, 158, 169-170, 181, 192, 195, 203

Dufty, Maely, 137, 168-170, 178, 183
Dufty, Bevan, 137, 178, 183
DuBois, W.E.B., 47, 109
Dylan, Bob, 57, 186, 201

Ebony, 147
Eckstine, Billy, 130-131, 178, 191
Eldridge, Roy, 40, 53, 106, 122, 136, 153
Errol Garner Trio, 152
Ethel Waters and Her Ebony Four, 11

Fagan, Sadie, 3-6, 8-10, 13, 15, 18, 21-24, 31, 38-39, 60, 77-78, 90, 109-110, 139, 166
FBI, 79
FBN, 96-97, 99-100, 116
The Father of Harlem, 19
Feather, Leonard, 76, 135, 166, 168, 176, 179
Feather, Lorraine, 5, 179, 194
Fisher, Alma, xiv
Flaps Record Shop, 13
Fletcher Henderson Band, 23, 31, 33, 38, 45, 53, 59
Fletcher Henderson and His Orchestra, 11
Forrest, Helen, 70, 72
Frederick Douglass High School, 9
French Quarters, 49

Garland, Judy, xviii, 116, 176
Garvey, Marcus Mosiah, 20
Gaye, Marvin, 186, 201
Gerry Mulligan Quartet, 152
The Genius of Ray Charles, 174
George Lewis Band, 151
Georgia on My Mind, 174
The George Shearing Quintet, 152
Gillespie, Dizzy, 68, 91, 118, 124, 132, 152, 159, 164, 186, 189,

200
Giuffre, Jimmy, 152
Golden Globe, 204
Goodman, Benny, 14, 35, 37, 40, 45, 47-48, 57, 67, 74, 77, 89, 95, 122,136,170
Gordy, Berry, 172
Gough, Phil, 8, 10
Granz, Norman, 103-104, 132, 156
Greenwich Village, 75, 94, 127, 166
Great Depression, 19, 24, 42-43, 47, 89
Green, Freddie, 61, 65, 86
Green, Nearest, 97-98
Greer, Sonny, 45
Gryce, Gigi, 152

Hackett, Bobby, 152
Hall Johnson and His Choir,106
Hall, Edmond, 65, 106
Hampton, Lionel, 95, 103, 108, 122, 183
Hanighen, Bernie, 36, 60
Hancock, Herbie, 199
Harlem Renaissance, 20-21
Harvard University, 60
Hardwick(e), Otto Toby, 45
Hawkins, Coleman, 45-48, 53, 108, 122, 153, 156, 162-163, 189, 200
Harris, Sara Julia, 2
Henderson, Bobby, 29-30, 37, 176
Henderson, Fletcher, 11, 23, 30-31, 33, 38, 45, 47, 53, 57, 59, 77, 86, 103, 200
Hendrix, Jimmie, 15
Heron, Gil Scott, 201
Herzog Jr., Arthur, 90, 135
Higginbotham, J.C., 33, 59
Hinds Agricultural High School, xvi
Hines, Earl, 40
Hoover, J. Edgar, 79
Hughes, Langston, 20, 82-83, 94

216

Holiday, Billie

Agent: Joe Glaser, 110, 114-115, 117, 125, 167, 170, 174, 176; **Albums:** *All or Nothing at All*, 202; *Body and Soul*; 202; *The Essential Billie Holiday*, 205; *Lady in Satin*, 205; *The Lady Sings*; 202; *The Legend of Billie Holiday*, 205; *Stay with Me*, 202; *Strange Fruit*, 205; *Velvet Mood*, 202; **Books:** *Lady Day: The Many Faces of Billie Holiday*, 17, 203; *Lady Sings the Blues*, 92, 109, 137, 141-142, 144-146, 148, 167, 172, 175, 180, 187, 204; **Broadway Production:** *Yesterdays: An Evening With Billie Holiday*; 203; **Husbands:** Jimmy Monroe; 90, 105, 107, 125; Louis McKay, xviii, 135, 141, 143-145, 149-150, 155, 157, 167-1968, 170, 172, 174, 180-181, 199; **Road Managers:** Joe Guy; 91-92, 109-110, 112-113, 117-118, 176; John Levy, 119, 124-129, 131, 135-136, 141, 150, 175; **Names:** Eleanora Harris; xiv; Eleanora Fagan; 1, 17; Eleanora McKay; 167; Lady Day, 17, 20-21, 38-40, 55, 57, 60, 73, 101, 105, 122, 134, 136-137, 139, 141, 145, 148-149, 151, 153-154, 156-159, 164, 167, 170, 178, 185, 188-190, 193-194, 198, 201, 203, 206; **Parents:** Sara Harris (Sadie Fagan); 3-6, 8-10, 13, 15, 18, 21-24, 31, 38-39, 60, 77-78, 90, 109-110, 139, 166; Clarence Holiday, 2-6, 8, 17-18, 23, 31, 44-45, 47, 59, 62-63, 86, 110, 139; **Stepparents:** Phil Gough; 8; Fannie Taylor Holiday, 18, 59, 63; **Songs:** *A Sunbonnet Blue and A Yellow Straw Hat*, 42; *Any Old Time*, 183; *Embraceable You*, 86, 202; *Farewell to Storyville*, 111; *Fine and Mellow*, 15, 86, 106, 136, 152, 154, 178, 187, 198; *He's Funny That Way*, 75, 142, 164; *How Am I to Know?* 86; *I Cover the Waterfront*, 86, 103, 136; *I Cried for You*, 75, 103; *I'll Get By*, 86; *I'm Gonna Lock My Heart*, 72; *I Gotta' Right to Sing the Blues*, 57; *I Wished on the Moon*, 57, 103; *Know What It Means to Miss New Orleans?* 111; *Lady Sings the Blues*, 180, 187, 195-197; *Love and Kisses*, 40; *Lover Come Back to Me*, 136, 199; *Lover Man*, 106, 108, 136, 202; *Mean to Me*, 66, 188; *Miss Brown to You*, 42, 57; *My Man*, 68, 103, 136, 145, 172, 180, 199; *My Old Flame*, 86; *Nightmare, Nightmare*, 183; *No Regrets*, 60; *Now or Never*, xix; *Out of Nowhere*, 183; *Riffin' the Scotch*, 37, 57; *Them There Eyes*, 75, 136, 148, 195; *Those Foolish Things*, 75; *Trav'lin All Alone*, 75; *Softly As in a Morning Sunrise*, 183; *Stormy Weather*, 30, 79, 199; *Summertime*, 52, 103; *This*

Year's Kisses, 66, 188; *Who Loves You,* 75; *Yesterdays,* 57, 86, 183, 199, 203; *and Your Mother's Son-In-Law,* 35, 57

Hollingsworth, Charles "Pod," 135
Hollon, Kenneth, 24, 26
Horace Silver Quintet, 152
Horne, Lena, 40, 79, 94, 102, 182, 189, 192
House of the Good Shepherd, 10, 17
Howard Theater, xiv, 41, 45, 61, 110
Huehl, Linda Lipnack, 17-18, 58, 120, 128, 177, 184, 191
Hurston, Zora Neale, 7, 20

International Jazz Day, 199

Jackson, Michael, xxi
James, Etta, xx, 79, 186
Jarreau, Al, 196
Jay-Z, 59, 163, 192
Jazz songs/tunes:
 Bye Bye Black Bird, 199; *I Love You For Sentimental Reasons,* 91; *It's Only a Paper Moon,* 91; *General Pilot,* 199; *Mr. Magic,* 199; *Somewhere Over the Rainbow,* 199; *Straighten Up and Fly Right,* 91; *Sweet Lorraine,* 91
JET Magazine, 136
Jimmy Smit Trio, 152
Johnson, Jack, 26-27
Johnson, Pete, 65, 77
Johnson, James Weldon, 20, 200
Jones, Jo, xviii, 65-67, 79, 86, 163, 178, 186, 200
Jones, Quincy, 98
Jungle Alley, 28-29, 33, 59

Khan, Chaka, 79
Kid Ory, 151
King Oliver Band, 26

Kuhn, Rolf, 152

Lafayette Theater, 25-26
Lamar, Kendrick, 201
Lansky, Meyer, 33
Larsen, Nella, 20
Lee, Canada, 106, 198
Lennon, John, 201
Let the Good Times Roll, 174
Lewis, Lux, 65
Lil Baby, 201
Lionel Hampton Houses, 183
The Littlest Rebel, 42
Locke, Allain, 20
Louis Armstrong & His Hot Five, 11
Louis Armstrong & His All-Stars, 151
Luciano, Lucky, 33

Maranzano, Salvatore, 33
Marley, Bob, 201
Marsalis, Wynton, 186-187, 190, 196
Mathews, Mat, 152
Marais Street, 50
McArthur, Alex, 193
Meredith, James, 195
Midgett, Memry, 132-133
Mills, Stephanie, 192
Millstein, Gilbert, 148
Mingus, Charles, 79, 98, 177, 200
McKay, Louis Jr., 180
McRae, Carmen, 152, 175, 178-179
Monterey Jazz Festival, 159
Moore, Ethel, 16-17
Morton, Benny, 106
Mulligan, Gerry, 152-153, 159

219

MusicalFare Theater, 193
Musician battle, 17

NAACP, vii, 77, 82, 84-85, 88, 109, 180
National Medal of Arts, 204
Nanton, Tricky Sam, 45
Nas, 192
Negro Movement, 21
New Bourbon Street Jazz Band of Jackson, Mississippi, 195
New Negro Movement, 21
New Haarlem, 19
New York Times, 1, 97-98, 124, 148
Nixon, Richard, 1
Noro Morales, 124
North Basin Street, 50
North Franklin Street, 50
North Robertson Street, 50
NWA, 148, 201

Oklahoma Blue Devils, 54
Oscar Peterson Trio, 152

Page, Walter, 65
Pan African Movement, 20
Paris, Jackie, 152
Parker, Charlie, 17-18, 47-48, 51, 91, 118, 123-124, 132, 140, 162-163, 183, 185, 189, 200
Payton Jr., Phillip, 19
Pinnock, Blondel A., 204
Pleasants, Henry, 197
Please Mr. Blues, 34
Pony Kane, 16

Protest songs:
    Oh, Freedom, 200; *Lift Every Voice and Sing,* 200;

Alabama Song, 200; *Strange Fruit,* 95, 127, 140-141, 174, 183, 201, 202; *Sixteen Tons,* 200; *We Shall Overcome,* 200; *Chain Gang,* 200; *The Times They Are A-Changing,* 201; *Mississippi Goddam,* 95, 201; *A Change is Gonna Come,* 201; *Say it Loud: I'm Black and I'm Proud,* 201; *Freedom Suite,* 201; *The Revolution Will Not Be Televised,* 201; *What's Going On,* 201; *Imagine,* 201; *I'll Take You There,* 201; *Get Up, Stand Up,* 201; *Born in the U.S.A.,* 201; *Fuck the Police,* 201; *Fight the Power,* 201; *Killing in the Name,* 201; *Revolution,* 201; *To Pimp a Butterfly,* 201; *Alright,* 201; *The Bigger Picture,* 201; *Riots: How Many Times,* 201; *Rockstar,* 201

Public Enemy, 201

Rage Against the Machine, 201
Raglin, Junior, 45
Rich, Buddy, 91
Rich, Wilbert, 10
Roach, Max, 51, 90-91, 159, 183, 189, 192
Robinson, Bill "Bojangles," 26, 32, 42-43
Rollins, Sonny, 5, 17-18, 108-109, 119, 144-145, 152, 159, 162-163, 189, 200
Rolling Stone Magazine, 204
Ross, Diana, 3, 18, 174, 180, 182, 196, 199, 204
Rush, Bobby, 8
Rushing, Jimmy, 61, 152
Rubin, Vanessa, 203

Seeger, Pete, 200
Shakur, Tupac, 140
Shaw, Artie, 14, 28, 60, 67, 69-72, 75, 104, 122, 135, 183
Skinny Davenport, 17-18
Sheridan Square, 75
Sherman, James, 65
Simone, Nina, 95, 172, 201
Smith, Bessie, 9, 11-13, 15, 17, 30, 32, 43-44, 47-48, 57, 63-64,

221

126, 160, 176
Smith, Buster, 54
Smith, Sussie, 4, 6
Smith, Stuff, 152
Stavers, Charlie, 106
Stewart, Slam, 106, 124
Sonny Stitt Quartet, 152
Springsteen, Bruce, 57, 201
Squeeze Inn, 8
St. Raymond's New Cemetery and Mausoleum, 206
The Staple Singers, 201
Stars of Jazz, 124, 145
Stan Kenton and His Orchestra, 152
Stewart, Rex William, 45
Swing Dat Hammer, 174
Symphony in Black, 40-42, 49

Tatum, Art, 2, 53, 106
Tawanna Shaunte, v., 186
Teagarden, Jack, 151
Teddy Wilson Trio, 152
Tizol, Juan, 45
Thomas, Franklin Augustus, 192
The Three Strings, 188
Trappier, Arthur, 106
Travis, Merle, 200
Treme Street, 50
Trey Songz, 201
The Three Millers, 25
Troup, Bobby, 145
Tucker, Bobby, 124-125, 155-156
Tuskegee Institute, 40

Ubandi Club, 57
United States v. Billie Holiday, 18, 117, 204

Vanderbilt Family Cemetery and Mausoleum, 178
Vaughan, Sarah, 1-2, 122, 133, 152, 182, 200
Vereen, Ben, 192
Verve Records, 132, 147, 156, 160, 176, 181
Villere Street, 50

The Yeah Man Club, 57
Young, Irma, 54
Young, Mary, 162
Young, Lee, 54
Young, Lester Willis, 37-40, 49, 53-54, 60-61, 64, 66-67, 73-74, 80, 86, 91, 98, 108, 122, 138, 148, 153-154, 158, 161-165, 171-172, 178, 184, 188-189, 193, 200, 205
Young, Lester Willis, Jr., 54, 184
Young, Lizetta, 53-54
Young, Willis Lester, 53-54, 158

Waldron, Mal, 153, 159
War on Drugs, 18, 52, 99-101, 169, 181, 204
Waters, Ethel, 11, 30, 47, 79, 82, 142, 160, 164
Webb, Chick, 3, 40, 68-69
Webster, Ben, 38, 40, 45, 106, 153, 156, 189, 200
Weill, Kurt, 200
White, Josh, 106
White, Sonny, 85, 90, 177
Wilbur de Paris, 152
Williams, Billy Dee, 18, 174, 180, 204
Winding, Kai, 152
Winehouse, Amy, 21, 186
Wilson, Cassandra, 186, 193
Wilson, Teddy, 18, 40, 42, 48, 50, 52, 67, 74, 77, 86, 110, 136
Wilson, William Llewellyn, 9
WJSU Jazz, 5, 198
Wright, Richard, 20, 94

Notes[129]

[1] David Margolick, *Strange Fruit*, p. 56.
[2] James Erstine. (2020). Billie. Billie - YouTube.
[3] Carl Schoettler, *Did Billie come from Philly, really*? The Baltimore Sun. Nov. 26, 1993.
[4] David Margolick, *Strange Fruit*, p. 68.
[5] Zora Neale Hurston. (1990) Tell My Horse: Voodoo and Life in Haiti and Jamaica. p. 9.
[6] Daniel Cross. 2016. I Am the Blues. Documentary. Watch I Am the Blues (2015) - Free Movies | Tubi (tubitv.com).
[7] Lost Your Head Blues Lost Your Head Blues lyrics - Search (bing.com).
[8] Me and My Gin Me and My Gin lyrics - Search (bing.com).
[9] Come Back, Sweet Papa by Louis Armstrong lyrics. LOUIS ARMSTRONG - COME BACK, SWEET PAPA LYRICS (songlyrics.com).
[10] Holiday, Billie & Dufty, William. (2006). *Lady Sings the Blues*. New York, New York, 11.
[11] James Erstine. (2020). Billie. Billie - YouTube.
[12] Billie Holiday and William Dufty. 2006. *Lady Sings the Blues*. P. 36.
[13] Artie Shaw. (1999). Billie's Blue Notes. *Newsweek*, 133 (26), p. 42.
[14] Ralph J. Gleason. *Celebrating the Duke*, p. 76.
[15] Ibid, p.75.
[16] Frank Jacobs. A Night Club Map of 1930s Harlem. Big Think. A Night-Club Map of 1930s Harlem - Big Think.
[17] Ibid. p. 105.
[18] Prohibition An Interactive History. The Speakeasies of the 1920s. The Speakeasies of the 1920s – Prohibition: An Interactive History (themobmuseum.org).
[19] Jack Doyle, 1939, p. 5
[20] Ralph J. Gleason. *Celebrating the Duke*, p. 56.
[21] David Margolick, *Strange Fruit*, p. 56.
[22] Ralph J. Gleason. *Celebrating the Duke*, p. 41.
[23] Malak Monir and Jessica Durando, USA Today, p. 2.
[24] Ibid, p. 43.
[25] Robert O'Meally. Lady Day: The *Many Faces of Lady Day*. p. 102.
[26] Billie Holiday – Riffin' The Scotch Lyrics | Genius Lyrics
[27] Jazz Time with Jarvis X. Sept. 8, 2020. Interview with Lester Young by Chris Albertson - August 24, 1958 - YouTube
[28] Billie Holiday - Saddest Tale Lyrics | SongMeanings
[29] David Margolick, *Strange Fruit*, p. 41.
[30] Ibid, p. 41.
[31] Ibid, p. 43.

[32] Pesala Bandara. (2017). The brothels, madams, and prostitutes of Storyville: America's only legal redlight district that closed 100 years ago. The brothels, madams and prostitutes of Storyville: America's only legal red-light district that closed 100 years ago - World News - Mirror Online. Daily Mirror.
[33] Genius. Carelessly. Billie Holiday – Carelessly Lyrics | Genius Lyrics
[34] Billie Holiday Summertime lyrics. Billie Holiday – Summertime Lyrics | Genius Lyrics
[35] James Erstine. (2020). Billie. Billie - YouTube.
[36] Genius. *No Regrets* – Billie Holiday 2022. Billie Holiday – No Regrets Lyrics | Genius Lyrics.
[37] Ibid. Interview of Jimmie Rowles.
[38] Carla Hay. Review 'Billie' (2020), An Oral History of Billie Holiday's Life. Culture Mix: Where Lifestyle Cultures Blend. Review: 'Billie' (2020), an oral history of Billie Holiday's life – CULTURE MIX (culturemixonline.com).
[39] Robert O'Meally. Lady Day: The *Many Faces of Lady Day*. p. 100.
[40] Musixmatch. Me, Myself, and I me, myself and I billie holiday lyrics - Search (bing.com).
[41] James Erstine. (2020). Billie. Billie - YouTube.
[42] Artie Shaw. June 28, 1999. *Billie's Blue Notes*. Newsweek. 133 (26), p. 42.
[43] Robert O'Meally. *Lady Day The Many Faces of Billie Holiday*. p. 127.
[44] Tracy Fessenden. (2019). Billie Full of Grace: How Billie Holiday learned to sing at the House of the Good Shepherd. NPR.
[45] Journalism of American History. (June 2011). Terrorism and the American Experience. Day 2. Terrorism on American Soil. Teaching the Journal of American History (oah.org).
[46] Ibid, p. 130.
[47] Nat Hentoff. *Jazz Is*. 1976. p. 54.
[48] Ralph J. Gleason. *Celebrating the Duke*, p. 80.
[49] James Erstine. (2020). Billie. Billie - YouTube.
[50] *The New York Times, Negro Cocaine 'Fiends' New Southern Menace*, Negro Cocaine Fiends - New Southern Menace - NYT February 8, 1914 (druglibrary.org).
[51] John White. (7 Feb. 2019). The History of Marijuana Prohibition in the U.S. The History of U.S. Marijuana Prohibition - CNBS.
[52] Johann Hari. (2016). *Chasing the Scream*, p. 36
[53] Ibid. p. 53.
[54] Johann Hari. (2016). *Chasing the Scream*, p. 19.
[55] Jack Dolye. (2021). Strange Fruit Book Review. PopHistoryDig.com
[56] John Szwed. (2015). *Billie Holiday: The Musician and the Myth*. p. 159.
[57] Genius. Strange Fruit Lyrics 2022. Billie Holiday – Strange Fruit Lyrics | Genius Lyrics.

58 John Szwed. (2015). *Billie Holiday: The Musician and the Myth*. p. 170.
59 The Billie Holiday Experience. Billie Holiday in "A New World A-Coming" (1944) - YouTube.
60 Irving Kahal and Sammy Fain. (2023). I'll Be Seeing You (1944) Single Version. Billie Holiday - I'll Be Seeing You [1944 Single Version] Lyrics | Lyrics.com.
61 Phone Interview with Sonny Rollins by Meredith Coleman McGee. June 1, 2023, 12 pm to 12:48 central; 1 pm to 1:48 pm eastern.
62 Phone Interview with Sonny Rollins by Meredith Coleman McGee. June 1, 2023, 12 pm to 12:48 central; 1 pm to 1:48 pm eastern.
63 Phone Interview with Sonny Rollins by Meredith Coleman McGee. June 1, 2023, 12 pm to 12:48 central; 1 pm to 1:48 pm eastern.
64 Phone Interview with Sonny Rollins by Meredith Coleman McGee. June 1, 2023, 12 pm to 12:48 central; 1 pm to 1:48 pm eastern.
65 Jazz Video Guy. April 18, 2018. Sonny Rollins: A Life in Jazz - YouTube.
66 Billie Holiday & William Dufty. *Lady Sings the Blues*, p. 121.
67 Billie Holiday & William Dufty. *Lady Sings the Blues*, p. 124.
68 Robert O'Meally. *Many Faces of Lady Day*. p. 148.
69 Farewell to Storyville lyrics. farewell to storyville lyrics - Search (bing.com).
70 Simon Hodgson. (2016). A Hell of a Businessman: A Biography of Joe Glaser.
71 Phone Interview with Sonny Rollins by Meredith Coleman McGee. June 1, 2023, 12 pm to 12:48 central; 1 pm to 1:48 pm eastern.
72 James Erstine. (2020). Billie. Billie - YouTube.
73 Billie Holiday and William Dufty. *Lady Sings the Blues*, p. 172-173.
74 Ibid. p. 183.
75 Oakland Tribune. (January 23, 1949). Singer Nabbed on Dope Charge. Pg. 23.
76 Johanne Hari. (2015). The Hunting of Billie Holiday. Politico. The Hunting of Billie Holiday - POLITICO Magazine.
77 I Found My Thrill On Blueberry Hill lyrics. https://www.bing.com/search?q=i+found+my+thrill+on+blueberry+hill+lyrics&cvid.
78 Lee Watkins (Bonnie) Adkins. Interview. March 30, 2023.
79 James Erskine. Billie. (2020). Billie - YouTube.
80 Billie Holiday, The Comeback Story. Billie Holiday in The Comeback Story - Bing video
81 Billie Holiday in Brussels. YouTube. Billie Holiday in Brussels (1954) - YouTube
82 Jet. (5 Aug. 1954). Billie Holiday's Ex-Mate Jailed As Bet Ring Kingpin, Crime.

[83] John Szwed. *Billie Holiday: The Musician and the Myth*. p. 23.
[84] Billie Holiday and William Dufty. *Lady Sings the Blues*, p. 223.
[85] Phone Interview with Sonny Rollins by Meredith Coleman McGee. June 1, 2023, 12 pm to 12:48 central; 1 pm to 1:48 pm eastern.
[86] Billie Holiday on Stars of Jazz. Billie Holiday on Stars of Jazz (1956) - YouTube.
[87] Joel Dinerstein. Lester Young and the Birth of Cool. *Academia* p. 250.
[88] The Billie Holiday Experience. The Greatest Broadcast Ever! - YouTube
[89] John Szwed. *Billie Holiday: The Musician and the Myth*. p. 51.
[90] John Szwed. *Billie Holiday: The Musician and the Myth*. p. 194.
[91] Interview with Lester Young By Christ Albertson. Recorded August 24, 1958 at WCAU, Philadelphia. Interview with Lester Young by Chris Albertson - August 24, 1958 - YouTube.
[92] Please Don't Talk About Me When I'm Gone song lyrics Billie Holiday - Please Don't Talk About Me When I'm Gone Lyrics | Lyrics.com
[93] François Postif. February 6, 1959. Lester in Paris - His last days - YouTube.
[94] Ferrini Productions. April 11, 2014. President of Beauty - YouTube.
[95] Loren Schoenberg. Lester's 1944 Three Little Words x 4 - YouTube.
[96] Phone Interview with Sonny Rollins by Meredith Coleman McGee. June 1, 2023, 12 pm to 12:48 central; 1 pm to 1:48 pm eastern.
[97] Joel Dinerstein. 27 Aug. 2009. Lester Young and the Birth of Cool. *Academia*. p. 242.
[98] Ibid. p. 252.
[99] Joel Dinerstein. Lester Young and the Birth of Cool. *Academia*. p. 240.
[100] Robert O'Meally. *Many Faces of Lady Day*. p. 194.
[101] Jody Rosen. Frank Sinatra and Billie Holiday: They Did It Their Way. The New York Times Style Magazine, 132.
[102] Leonard Feather's 1966 release "Encyclopedia of Jazz in the 60's." C Jam Blues - Earl Fatha Hines & Johnny Hodges - YouTube
[103] Bessie Smith 1895 – 1937. Bessie Smith | National Museum of African American History and Culture.
[104] Peter Allsopp. The Estate of Billie Holiday – In many sad ways reflects her life. The Estate of Billie Holiday — in many sad ways reflects her life | by Peter Allsopp | Medium.
[105] Peter Keepnews. Feb. 8, 2023. Sylvia Syms, Versatile British Actress, Is Dead at 89. *New York Times*. Sylvia Syms, Versatile British Actress, Is Dead at 89 - The New York Times (nytimes.com).
[106] James Erskine. Billie. (2020). Billie - YouTube.
[107] Seisdedos Garcia. (2022). Admad Jamal, 'You turn on the TV and never see Billie Holiday… that's when you know the world isn't doing well." El Pais. Ahmad Jamal, pianist: 'You turn on the TV and never see

Billie Holiday… that's when you know the world isn't doing well' (msn.com).
[108] Jazz Video Guy. April 18, 2018. Sonny Rollins: A Life in Jazz - YouTube.
[109] L. Rothman. Billie Holiday's Story Was Ever More Complicated Than You Think. *Time.com*. N1.
[110] David Radlauer. The Real Billie Holiday, Part One – 1930s. Jan. 31, 2022. *The Syncopated Times*, The Real Billie Holiday, Part One – 1930s - The Syncopated Times.
[111] Christopher Loudon, The voice that launched a thousand voices. Maclean's, p. 72.
[112] Tracy Fessenden. Billie Full of Grace: How Billie Holiday learned to sing at the House of the Good Shephard. NRP.
[113] James Erskine. Billie. (2020). Billie - YouTube.
[114] Annika Holmberg. Sept. 11, 2022. Billie Holiday's Last Home, a Stately Upper West Side Brownstone, Looks for $14M - DailyDEEDS (cottagesgardens.com).
[115] Nicole Duncan-Smith. Billie Holiday as activist: Can a movie change the singer's image? *Christian Science Monitor*. 08827729.
[116] Aida Amoako. *Strange Fruit: The most shocking song of all time?* BBC.
[117] Nat Hentoff. (1972). *Jazz Is*. A Ridge Press Book. p. 57.
[118] Lorraine Feather. Interview. January 23, 2023.
[119] Ron Welch. Interview. April 4, 2023. Jazz with Raphael Semmes Quartet in The Dining Room at Hal & Mals, Jackson, Mississippi.
[120] Black History: Billie Holiday's "Strange Fruit." (2021). Black History: Billie Holiday's "Strange Fruit" - African American News and Issues (aframnews.com).
[121] Schuyler Manning. Interview. Tuesday, April 11, 2023. Jazz with Raphael Semmes Quartet in The Dining Room at Hal & Mals, Jackson, Mississippi.
[122] Lady Sings the Blues lyrics. billie holiday lady sings the blues 1956 lyrics - Search (bing.com).
[123] Robert Christgau. June 9, 2005. The First Lady of Song. The First Lady of Song (thenation.com).
[124] Cloe Rabinowitz. (2023). *Drea Dominque Releases Rendition of Billie Holiday's Classic 'I'll Be Seeing You*.' Broadway World Music. Drea Dominique Releases Rendition of Billie Holiday's Classic 'I'll Be Seeing You' (broadwayworld.com).
[125] Shirley Shaw Bracey. Interview. Tuesday, April 25, 2023. Jazz with Raphael Semmes Quartet in The Dining Room at Hal & Mals, Jackson, Mississippi.

Billie Holiday: Jazz Singer

[126] 2023 International Jazz Day All-Star Global Concert, April 30, 2023. Facebook
[127] Billie Holiday Album Sales. 2023. BILLIE HOLIDAY album sales (bestsellingalbums.org)
[128] Carnegie Hall Icons. Billie Holiday Jazz Singer. Billie Holiday | Carnegie Hall
[129] 2023 International Jazz Day All Star Concert. April 30, 2023. https://www.facebook.com/herbiehancock/videos/768987478224188/.

229

Bibliography

Arts Meme. (2015). Billie Holiday in Los Angeles: the blues were brewing. March 20, 2023 <u>Billie Holiday in Los Angeles: the blues were brewing | arts•meme (artsmeme.com)</u>.

Augustyn, Adam. (August 21, 2022). Billie Holiday American Jazz Singer, *Encyclopaedia Britannica*.

The Baltimore Sun. (2022). Billie's Story.

BBC. May 29, 2012.
<u>1959 The Year that Changed Jazz - YouTube</u>.

Billie Holiday Documentary. From the BBC 'Reputations' Series. (2020.) <u>Billie Holiday Documentary ('From the BBC 'Reputations' Series) - YouTube</u>

Billie Holiday With Count Basie and His Orchestra – Swing Brother Swing. (2012). <u>Billie Holiday With Count Basie & His Orchestra - Swing Brother Swing - YouTube</u> Grammercy Records.

The Billie Holiday Experience. WMCA-FM Radio Broadcast. June 25, 1944. <u>Billie Holiday in "A New World A-Coming" (1944) - YouTube</u>.

The Billie Holiday Theater. *Our Story*. Jan. 7, 2023.
<u>The Billie Holiday Theatre - THE BILLIE HOLIDAY THEATRE</u>

Biography. Billie Holiday 1915-1959. (Nov. 15, 2022).
<u>Billie Holiday - Movie, Death & Strange Fruit</u>

(biography.com).

Black Heritage Commemorative Society. (2011). Billie Holiday. March 10, 2023, Billie Holiday Biography at Black History Now - Black Heritage Commemorative Society.

Blair, Elizabeth. (2012). The Strange Story of the Man Behind 'Strange Fruit': NPR. The Strange Story Of The Man Behind 'Strange Fruit': NPR.

Butler, Gerry. (2007). Billie Holiday 1915-1959. Black Past. Dec. 11, 2022 Billie Holiday (1915-1959) • (blackpast.org).

Campbell, Craig. (27 March 2019). The Sunday Post. March 2, 2023 The story of Billie Holiday, part one: A child of poverty, a daughter of teen parents, a woman who defined jazz - The Sunday Post.

Carrillo, Juanita Karen. How Billie Holiday's 'Strange Fruit' Confirmed and Ugly Era of Lynchings. History Stories. History. (May 10, 2021). How Billie Holiday's 'Strange Fruit' Confronted an Ugly Era of Lynchings - HISTORY.

Chase, Anthony. (2023). Excellent vocals propel Billie Holiday musical 'Lady Day' at MusicalFare. *Buffalo News*. Excellent vocals propel Billie Holiday musical 'Lady Day' at MusicalFare (buffalonews.com).

Christgau, Robert. (June 9, 2005) The First Lady of Song. *The Nation*. March 15, 2023 The First Lady of Song | The Nation.

Columbia Electronic Encyclopedia. (2021). *John Henry Hammond*. 6th edition. p. 1.

Columbia Records History. (2022). Columbia Records Company History Timeline. November 8, 2022. online.

Daniels, Douglas Henry. (2008). Lester Leaps In: The Life and Times of Lester Young University of California Television. Lester Leaps In: The Life and Times of Lester Young - YouTube

Davies, Russell. (2005). 'Birdsong' The Charlie Parker Story. Birdsong: The Charlie Parker Story - BBC Radio (2005) - YouTube

Davis, Francis. (Nov. 2000). Our Lady of Sorrows. *Atlantic Monthly*, 104-108.

Dieterle, Marcus. (2023). Baltimore Center Stage's next season to feature productions about Billie Holiday, Cinderella, and more. Retrieved online April 4, 2023 from, Baltimore Center Stage announces 2023/2024 season (baltimorefishbowl.com).

Dinerstein, Joel. (1998). Lester Young and the Birth of Cool, *Academia*. 239-276.

Discography of American Historical Recordings, s.v. "Columbia matrix W148064. My kinda love / Fletcher Henderson's Orchestra," accessed March 11, 2023, https://adp.library.ucsb.edu/index.php/matrix/detail/2000037626/W148064-My_kinda_love.

Doyle, Jack (1939). *Strang Fruit*, Music, Biography, Civil Rights. 1-13.

Duncan-Smith, Nicole. (5 March 2021). Billie Holiday as activist: Can a movie change the singer's image?

Christian Science Monitor, 08827729.

Encyclopaedia Britannica. Apollo Theater. (February 9, 2023). Apollo Theater | History, Performers, & Facts | Britannica.

Encyclopaedia Britannica. *Charlie Parker*. Assessed Jan. 21, 2013 Charlie Parker -- Britannica Online Encyclopedia.

Encyclopaedia Britannica. Cotton Club. (March 28, 2023). Cotton Club | Description, History, & Facts | Britannica.

Encyclopaedia Britannica. *Ella Fitzgerald*. (Nov. 02, 2022). Ella Fitzgerald | Biography, Music, & Facts | Britannica.

Encyclopaedia Britannica. (2023). Jack Johnson. (March 28, 2023). Jack Johnson | Biography, Record, Pardon, & Facts | Britannica.

Encyclopaedia Britannica. (2023). *Motown American corporation*. Motown -- Britannica Online Encyclopedia.

Encyclopaedia Britannica. (2017). Storyville. April 9, 2023. Storyville -- Britannica Online Encyclopedia.

Encyclopdia.com. (2018). Lester Young 1909 – 1959. Lester Young | Encyclopedia.com.

Erskine, James. *Billie*. (2020). Billie - YouTube.

Fessenden, Tracy. (20 Aug. 2019). Billie Full of Grace: How Billie Holiday learned to sing at the House of Good Shepherd. NPR. Singing For Eternity: Billie Holiday At The House Of The Good Shepherd: NPR.

Finn, Natalie. (2021). The infuriating True Story Behind *The United States vs. Billie Holiday*. Retrieved online April 23,

2022 from, The True Story Behind The United States vs. Billie Holiday - E! Online (eonline.com).

Garcia, Seisdedos. (2022). Admad Jamal, 'You turn on the TV and never see Billie Holiday… that's when you know the world isn't doing well." El Pais. MSN. Ahmad Jamal, pianist: 'You turn on the TV and never see Billie Holiday… that's when you know the world isn't doing well' (msn.com).

Genius. No Regrets – Billie Holiday (2022). Retrieved online December 4, 2022, from Billie Holiday – No Regrets Lyrics | Genius Lyrics.

Gleason, Ralph J. *Celebrating the Duke: And Louis, Bessie, Billie, Bird, Carmen, Miles, Dizzy and Other Heroes*. Boston, Massachusetts: Da Capo Press, 1995.

Hari, Johann. *Chasing the Scream: The First and Last Days of the War on Drugs*. Bloomsbury Publishing. New York: New York, 2016.

Hari, Johann. (2015). The Hunting of Billie Holiday. *Politico*. The Hunting of Billie Holiday - POLITICO Magazine. Harlem Jazz Clubs: 1920-40 – The Harlem Neighborhood Block Association (hnba.nyc). image Harlem Jazz Clubs 12=1920-1940.

Hathaway, Heather. (2003). *Strange Fruit: Billie Holiday, Café Society, and an Early Cry for Civil Rights. African American Review*, 37(1), 154-155.

Hay, Carla. Review: 'Billie' (2020), An Oral History of Billie Holiday. Culture Mix: Where Lifestyle Cultures Blend. Retrieved Jan. 22, 2023 from, Review: 'Billie' (2020), an oral history of Billie Holiday's life – CULTURE MIX (culturemixonline.com).

Hentoff, Nat. *Jazz Is*. Random House. New York: New York, 1976.

Heuchan, Claire. (2021). The United States vs. Billie Holiday Erases Her Bisexuality. November 18, 2022 https://afterellen.com/the-united-states-vs-billie-holiday-erases-her-bisexuality/.

Hodgson. Simon. (2016). *A Hell of a Businessman: A Biography of Joe Glaser.* Words on Play. A.C.T. Retrieved online January 14, 2023 from A Hell of a Businessman: A Biography of Joe Glaser (act-sf.org).

Holmberg, Annika. Sept. 11, 2022. Billie Holiday's Lase Home, a Stately Upper West Side Brownstone, Looks for $14M. Retrieved online May 7, 2023 from DailyDEEDS. Billie Holiday's Last Home, a Stately Upper West Side Brownstone, Looks for $14M - DailyDEEDS (cottagesgardens.com).

Indiana History Blog. (18 April 2023). *From Strange Fruit to Seeds of Change?: The Aftermath of the Marion Lynching.* From Strange Fruit to Seeds of Change?: The Aftermath of the Marion Lynching – The Indiana History Blog.

Indiana History Blog. (18 April 2023). *Strange Fruit: The 1930 Marion Lynching and the Woman Who Tried to Prevent It*. Strange Fruit: The 1930 Marion Lynching and the Woman Who Tried to Prevent It – The Indiana History Blog

Indianapolis Reporter. (16 Aug. 1930). *Scene of Thursday's Double Lynching Orgy Again Tranquil With Presence of State Guards, Who Brought Peace To The Mob City.*

Pgs. 1, 8.

Jacobs. Frank. (2010). A Night Club Map of 1930s Harlem. Big. Think. A Night-Club Map of 1930s Harlem - Big Think.

Jazz Time with Jarvis X. Interview with Lester Young by Christ Albertson. Recorded August 24, 1958, at WCAU-FM radio, Philadelphia. Interview with Lester Young by Chris Albertson - August 24, 1958 - YouTube.

Jazz by Decade: 1930-1740. (2019). *How Jazz Gave Rise to Swing in the 1930s*. October 2, 2022.

Jazz Video Guy. July 6, 2010.
Sonny Rollins: What Jazz Is, and What Being a Jazz Musician Means To Me - YouTube.

Jazz Video Guy. April 18, 2018.
Sonny Rollins: A Life in Jazz - YouTube.

Jazz Video Guy. June 4, 2012.
Sonny Rollins Remembers Ben Webster, Pres and Hawk - YouTube.

Joseph. A Jazz Music Timeline: From The Beginning to Today. (Oct. 18, 2022). April 6, 2023 A Jazz Music Timeline: From the Beginning to Today (walnutcreekband.org).

Journalism of American History. (June 2011). Terrorism and the American Experience. Day 2. Terrorism on American Soil. Teaching the Journal of American History (oah.org).

Kennedy, William. (2022). *The Truth and Myth Behind The 1937 Death of Bessie Smith.* Grunge.

Kline, Sidney. Billie Holiday Meets Last Cue, Dies at 44. Publication unknown.

Loudon, Christopher. (4, 6, 2015). The voice that launched a thousand voices. *Maclean's*. 128 (13/14), 72.

Lund & Co. Lester Young's Life: His personal life. February 21, 2023 Lesteryoung.dk - His Personal Life.

Major, Brian. (2020). Before Charlie Parker, there was Lester Young. Retrieved March 22, 2023, from *Swalawag* Magazine. Before Charlie Parker, there was Lester Young – Scalawag (scalawagmagazine.org).

Margolick, David. (2001). *Strange Fruit*, The Ecco Press, NY: New York.

Marshall, Colin. *Cabaret Cards: The Law Police Used to Keep Musicians of Color Off Stage*. WBGO and Jazz at Lincoln Center. Cabaret Cards: The Law Police Used To Keep Musicians Of Color Off Stage: NPR.

Mayor de Blascio Signs Legislation to Repeal Cabaret Law. (2017). De Blasio Signs Legislation Repealing Cabaret Law That Banned Dancing At Many Bars, Restaurants - CBS New York (cbsnews.com).

Merlis, Bob, and Seay, Davin. (2004). *Heart & Soul: A Celebration of Black Music Style in America 1930-1975*. Burlington, Vermont: Verve Editions.

Monir, Malak and Durando, Jessica. *USA Today*. Online. April 7, 2015, 1-5.

Newport Jazz Festival 1957 Setlists. March 2, 2023 Newport Jazz Festival 1957 Setlists | setlist.fm.

Nearest Green Foundation. (2019). About Nearest Green. March 19, 2023 ABOUT NEAREST GREEN | NEAREST GREEN.

The New York Times. (8 Feb. 1914). *Negro Cocaine 'Fiends' New Southern Menace*, Negro Cocaine Fiends - New Southern Menace - NYT February 8, 1914 (druglibrary.org).

National Museum of African American History & Culture. 2023. Bessie Smith 1895 – 1937. Bessie Smith | National Museum of African American History and Culture.

O'Meally, Robert. *Lady Day: The Many Faces of Billie Holiday*. NY, New York: Arcade Publishing, 1991.

Paramount Pictures. (1935). Symphony in Black: A Rhapsody of Negro Life. https://www.youtube.com/watch?v=LPD-8-I68L4.

Please Kill Me. *Inside Café Society: NYC's First Integrated Nightclub*. Retrieved Dec. 21, 2021 from, INSIDE CAFÉ SOCIETY: NYC'S FIRST INTEGRATED NIGHTCLUB (pleasekillme.com).

Postif, François. February 6, 1959. Lester in Paris - His last days - YouTube.

Promipool. (2023). These Were Harry Belafonte's Wives. THESE Were Harry Belafonte's Wives! (msn.com).

Rabinowitz, Cloe. (2023). *Drea Dominque Releases Rendition of Billie Holiday's Classic 'I'll Be Seeing You*.' Broadway World Music. Drea Dominique Releases Rendition of Billie Holiday's Classic 'I'll Be Seeing You' (broadwayworld.com).

Radlauer, David. The Real Billie Holiday, Part One – 1930s. April 4, 2023 The Syncopated Times, The Real Billie Holiday, Part One – 1930s - The Syncopated Times.

Reney, Tom. Lester Young: From Woodville to Algiers to Minneapolis to Kansas City. *New England Public Media*. February 20, 2023 Lester Young: From Woodville to Algiers to Minneapolis to Kansas City (nepm.org).

Ronk, Liz, Aneja, Arpita; and Berman, Eliza. Wynton Marsalis Recalls Billie Holiday on 100th Anniversary of Her Birth. *Time.com*. April 6, 2015. p. N1.

Rosen, Jody. (2015). Frank Sinatra and Billie Holiday: They Did It Their Way. *New York Times Style Magazine*, 132.

Salem Press Biographical Encyclopedia. (2021). Billie Holiday. Salem, D.C., 4 pgs.

Sam Gilford Music Videos. June 10, 2016. Lester Young Story of Pres 1. lester Young-StoryOfPres1 - YouTube.

Sam Gilford Music Videos. June 10, 2016. Lester Young-StoryOfPres4 - YouTube.

Saxton, Theda Palmer. (2022). Bill's Place, Speakeasies, and Billie Holiday on Swing Street. Retrieved, March 10, 2023 from, Routes: A Guide to African American Culture, Bill's Place, Speakeasies and Billie Holiday on Swing Street (routes-mag.com).

Schoettler, Carl. (Nov. 26, 1993). Did Billie come from Philly, really? The Baltimore Sun.

Segal, Corinne. (2016). This flag once protested lynching. No it's an artist's response to police violence. PBS News Weekend. Retrieved April 7, 2023 from PBS News Weekend. This flag once protested lynching. Now it's an artist's response to police violence | PBS News Weekend.

Shaw, Artie. (1999). Billie's Blue Notes. *Newsweek*, 133(*26*), p. 42.

Song Meaning. (2023). *Saddest Tale: Billie Holiday.* March 12, 2023 Billie Holiday - Saddest Tale Lyrics | SongMeanings.

Spartacus Educational. (2022). Abel Meeropol. Oct. 16, 2022 Abel Meeropol (spartacus-educational.com).

Sundrival, Diksha. (2020). Were Hattie McDaniel and Tallulah Bankhead in a Relationship? TheCinemaholic.

The Syncopated Times. (2020). *Duke Ellington and his Cotton Club Orchestra*. Retrieved March 28, 2023 from, Duke Ellington and his Cotton Club Orchestra - The Syncopated Times.

Szalavitz, Maia (13 Dec. 2015). Vice News. Online. A Brief History of New York City's Heroin Scene (vice.com)

Szwed, John. *Billie Holiday: The Musician and the Myth*, New York: NY, Penguin Books.

Time. 1939: Billie Holiday. (2020). 100 Women of the Year. World. Billie Holiday: 100 Women of the Year | Time

10 Things You Should Know About Ethel Waters - YouTube. Oct. 30, 2021.

Vitale, Tom (27 Aug. 2009). Lester Young: 'The Prez' Still Rules at 100. NPR. Morning Edition.

UNESCO and Herbie Hancock Institute of Jazz. (2023). 2023 International Jazz Day All-Star Global Concert. https://www.facebook.com/herbiehancock/videos/768987478224188/.

Ward, Geoffrey C. (1994). Billie Holiday. *American Heritage*, 9(*45*), 8, 14-16.

Waters, Ethel and Samuels, Charles. *His Eye Is On The Sparrow*. Cambridge, MA: Da Capo Press.

West Philadelphia Collaborative History. (Dec. 11, 2022). West Philadelphia Collaborative History - The Philadelphia General Hospital: From Almshouse to Public Hospital and Beyond (upenn.edu).

White, John. (7 Feb. 2019). *The History of Marijuana Prohibition in the U.S.* CNBS. The History of U.S. Marijuana Prohibition - CNBS.

WKCR 89.9 FM. (2022). Lester Young and Charlie Parker: Birthday Festival. Columbia University. Lester Young & Charlie Parker Festival | WKCR 89.9FM NY (columbia.edu).

World History Education. (2020). *Billie Holiday: Facts and Greatest Achievements*. January 8, 2023 Billie Holiday: Facts and Greatest Achievements - World History Edu.

www.ingramcontent.com/pod-product-compliance
Lightning Source LLC
Chambersburg PA
CBHW011521070526
44585CB00022B/2493